# Lethal Aspects of Urban Violence

# Lethal Aspects of Urban Violence

Edited by
**Harold M. Rose**
University of Wisconsin–Milwaukee

**Lexington Books**
D.C. Heath and Company
Lexington, Massachusetts
Toronto

50421

**Library of Congress Cataloging in Publication Data**

Main entry under title:

Lethal aspects of urban violence.

1. Homicide—United States—Congresses. 2. Cities and towns—United States—Congresses. 3. Violence—United States—Congresses. I. Rose, Harold M.

HV6529.L47                 364.1'52                 77-18680

ISBN 0-669-02117-2

Published simultaneously in Canada.

Printed in the United States of America.

International Standard Book Number: 0-669-02117-2

Library of Congress Catalog Card Number: 77-18680

# Contents

# Editor's Preface

Levels of lethal violence have increased several-fold in large urban environments during the past decade. Numerous surveys indicate that there is growing fear on the part of segments of the population who reside in large cities that selected urban environments constitute zones of danger. It is believed that these perceptions are greatly influenced by media reports on the frequency of the commission of acts of violence. Police departments, with the assistance of external funding, have initiated programs designed to alleviate facets of the problem of increasing acts of interpersonal violence. But most people, it appears, view this problem both as inevitable and intractable. It is assumed that it will probably run its course and eventually dissipate as a result of internal change rather than through external intervention efforts. We happen to disagree with the latter position and are proponents of the development of interventionist strategies designed to reduce the scope and magnitude of the problem. However, before logical design strategies can be introduced that may prove effective, it is imperative that we disaggregate the problem in ways that might enhance the possibility of lessened risk. Thus, the essays presented here represent a first attempt to bring together a small group of social scientists and members of the legal and medical profession to assess the current state of the problem—an important first step enroute to the formulation of interventionist strategies.

To facilitate the bringing together of persons known to be interested in the problem, a conference was held on May 15 and 16, 1977. The conference participants included the contributors to this volume; paper discussants; session convenors; and an invited group of professionals whose jobs were somehow related to specific aspects of the problem. The two-day session proved to be productive in assisting the various interest groups in initiating discussions across disciplinary and service-provider lines. Most of the papers appearing in this volume have undergone some revision, as a result of conference input. Only two of the papers included in this volume were not formally presented at the conference. The Overview and the paper entitled "Black Women and Homicide" were not among those scrutinized by conference participants. It is hoped that the conference established a small network of interdisciplinary social scientists and legal and medical scholars who will continue to communicate with each other as a means of shedding additional light on problems of mutual interest.

Besides those persons whose contributions appear in this volume, a number of other persons made significant input to the conference as a result of their critical comments and assessments of the problem in an alternative context. The primary representatives of this contributor group were Dr. Richard Henry (Univ. of Wisconsin-Milwaukee, Sociology); Dr. Ronald K. Wright, M.D. (Deputy Chief Medical Examiner, Dade County, Florida); Dr. Reynolds Farley (Univ. of Michigan, Sociology); Dr. Jose Hernandez (Univ. of Wisconsin-Milwaukee,

Sociology); Dr. Floyd Stoner (Marquette University, Political Science); Dr. Ernest Spaights (Univ. of Wisconsin-Milwaukee, Educational Psychology) Dr. Pearl M. Dansby (Tennessee State University, Psychology); Dr. Eugene Eisman (Univ. of Wisconsin-Milwaukee, Psychology); Dr. Richard H. Patterson, M.D. (Private Practice—Psychiatry); and Professor Flora Bryant (Univ. of Wisconsin-Milwaukee, Social Work).

Much effort was invested in developing and organizing the conference out of which these essays in their final form evolved. The Urban Research Center at the University of Wisconsin-Milwaukee graciously agreed to provide financial support to sponsor the conference and also provided typing and other forms of assistance which were critical to the development of a successful conference. I am especially indebted to Dr. Ann L. Greer, Director of the Center, whose idea it was that we develop such a conference, and to Mr. Jan Swatek, Assistant Center Director, who assumed the full responsibility for the financial management for the conference. And finally, I would like to extend special thanks to Ms. Lynn Roback, my research assistant, who undertook the task of working out all of the conference details, including communications with all conference participants, without whose help the conference would not have run so smoothly, and this set of essays might never have been produced.

# PRESENTING G.Q. LIVE . . . .

*A Showcase of the Best in Men's Fashion.*

*Bloomingdale's and
Gentleman's Quarterly Magazine
cordially invite you to
GQ Live, a fashion show and
cocktail reception.*

*Sunday, September 21st, 7pm, Bloomingdale's 2nd floor.
Tickets will be available at the door.*

## AROUND THE U.S.

# North Carolina killer-rapist is executed

Associated Press

RALEIGH, N.C. — A man who raped and killed a woman was executed Friday less than a mile from where he terrorized his victim and left her to bleed to death. John William Rook was put to death by injection at the Central Prison for the slaying of nurse Ann Marie Roche, who was raped, beaten, slashed and run over by a car before being left to die on May 12, 1980. Rook was the 16th person executed this year in the United States. Rook's final words were: "Freedom, freedom at last, man! It's been a good one."

Special Group Men's
Long Sleeve Authentic

## Western Shirts

by
Famous
Makers
Values To
31.98

# McDonald gets ten years in shooting

DURANT - Johnny McDonald of Cartwright, charged with shooting with intent to kill, was found guilty Tuesday by a District Court jury of assault and battery with a dangerous weapon.

The jury assessed his sentence at 10 years. Sentencing was set for Oct. 20.

McDonald was charged with shooting Guy McVeigh in the jaw on May 11 with a .45 caliber Curtz automatic.

McVeigh has since died from an accidental gunshot wound that occurred when a gun he was cleaning fell and discharged.

Assistant District Attorney Theresa McGehee used the transcript of McVeigh's sworn testimony during McDonald's preliminary hearing.

iley. Mrs. Barnett, who suff
ary hypertension, cannot have the requ
r family and friends can come up wit

ngful death suit

The New

"First I

to sell some assets

Page 3

e, Zuma Cleaves,
geles; 11 grandchildren;
at-grandchildren; and
e great-great
ildren.

Okla., wi...
day in Johns
with the Rev
ficiating. Bur

# Crime spree over as suspect kills himself

By TOM COHEN
Associated Press writer

WRIGHT CITY, Mo. — Residents haunted by the presence of fugitive Michael Wayne Jackson relaxed today after the suspect in a three-state crime spree killed himself when he was cornered by police in an abandoned barn.

"We can finally unload our shotguns," said resident Nelson Paul, 28, as he stood in the rain outside a police command center early today. "It's like having a load of bricks lifted from your shoulder.

Jackson, a 41-year-old former mental patient, shot himself in the head late Thursday with the same shotgun he had used throughout the rampage that began Sept. 22 and left three people dead, said Hal Helterhoff, head of the FBI office in St. Louis.

"We're pleased to bring peace and quiet back to Wright City," Helterhoff said at a news conference today. "You always get very pleased when you can bring a menace to society to final justice."

## Norman Eugene Clark

DALLAS — Funeral for Norman Eugene Clark, 38, former Denison resident who was found dead Friday in his Dallas taxi cab after being robbed and stabbed, will be at 11 a.m. Thursday in Nat Clark Funeral Home in Dallas, 3100 Dently Dr. Burial will be in Grand Prairie.

Clark was born Nov. 10, 1947, in Denison. He attended Terrell School, graduating May 31, 1966. In July 1966, Clark enlisted in the Army, being honorably discharged in 1970. He was a Vietnam veteran and a graduate of Eastfield College. Clark had completed 200 hours of classroom instruction in carpentry and was also an automotive finisher. He was a teacher at Brookshire College.

Surviving are his mother, Delphine Thomas of Denison; father, Melvin of New York City; two daughters, Nicole Strewther of Denison, Michelle Clark of Dallas; and three sisters of New York City.

The family will be at 4016 Civil Hill Dr.

that he had slain someone, county sheriff's dispatcher Bob Gresham Jr. said Wednesday.

Long "didn't come out and say, 'I killed three girls,'" Gresham said. "The jailer said that guy out there was talking about killing somebody, as in past tense. But people say that sort of thing all the time."

Lancaster Police Chief John Whitehead said Long had $3 in Dallas.

Goodbye, get out of my county."

A murder warrant was issued Wednesday for the 34-year-old Bay City man, who police say was staying at the house in this Dallas suburb where a blind invalid, her cousin and a transient were hacked to death.

Long was charged with capital murder in a warrant signed by a state district judge in Dallas.

will appear telling somebody,

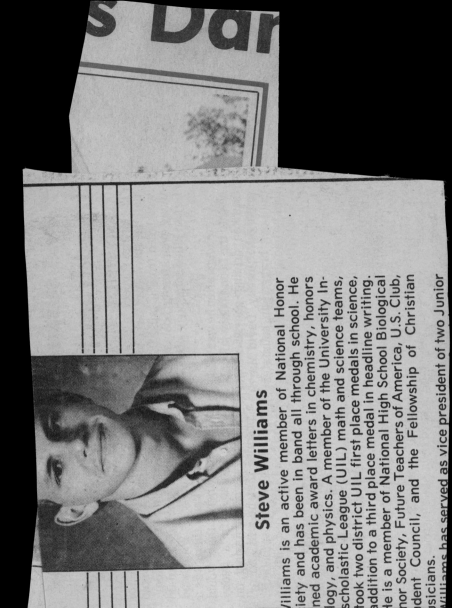

## Steve Williams

Williams is an active member of National Honor
iety and has been in band all through school. He
ned academic award letters in chemistry, honors
logy, and physics. A member of the University In-
scholastic League (UIL) math and science teams,
took two district UIL first place medals in science.
addition to a third place medal in headline writing.
He is a member of National High School Biological
nor Society, Future Teachers of America, U.S. Club,
dent Council, and the Fellowship of Christian
usicians.

Williams has served as vice president of two Junior

ere it was thought Jackson, a
crime spree, was hiding.

# Lethal Aspects of Urban Violence

# 1

## Lethal Aspects of Urban Violence: An Overview

*Harold M. Rose*

Violence in urban America is of interest to almost everyone. For violence manifests itself in numerous ways. For some, contact with violence is simply the constant dosage that is transmitted via television, while for others the constant fear of personal injury and/or the loss of material goods attest to the perceived level of violence which exists within some residential neighborhoods. While violence manifests itself in many forms and degrees of seriousness, the principal concern of this set of essays is the varying facets of the violence syndrome which end in death. Thus, the essays which appear in this volume will focus upon one or more facets of the increasingly serious national homicide problem.

Homicide, unlike other behavioral causes of death, seldom receives extensive attention by social science scholars, although it is frequently a topic of treatment by novelists and other writers of fiction. A more recent review of the literature, however, tends to indicate a renewal of interest in the subject by a growing number of social science and medical scholars. This renewed interest stems in part from the recent increase in the magnitude of homicide deaths in the nation and a growing recognition that serious effort should be devoted to attempts to reduce the magnitude of the problem. However, there are still those who do not view homicide as the kind of problem for which intervention is feasible, nor should strenuous efforts be made to bring it under control. The latter position was recently expressed by Bruce-Briggs in his argument against efforts at gun control. Briggs comments on this issue in the following way:

> Firearms are rarely employed for rape, home burglary, or street muggings. On the other hand, a good portion of the most heinous crime, murder, is not a serious source of social fear. The majority of murders are the result of passionate argument, and although personal tragedies are not a social concern—ditto for crimes committed by criminals against one another.[1]

The implication of this argument is that the victims of homicide are seldom people who count, and thus the cost of curtailing the incidence of homicide may exceed its value. The latter position aside, efforts are being made to both reduce the incidence and lessen the burden on surviving kin.

The impact of homicide on society is indeed complex. The dyadic interaction that leads to death imposes a variety of costs upon society. These costs are social, psychological, and economic. There have been few efforts to measure the costs of these tragic events. Nuclear families are dissolved, siblings are lost,

and dependency is intensified. Offenders are charged, convicted, and imprison-
ed at public expense. Given the low median age at which most homicides occur,
the number of potential working years lost is high. Thus, the psychological
trauma resulting from the sudden and unexpected loss of a loved one, the
possibility of increased economic dependency, and the resulting stress associated
with these acts suggest that we take a new look at this phenomenon. This new
look should attempt to illustrate the complex linkages and their implications
for society that grow out of the lethality associated with the rising incidence
of violence.

## Homicide and the Urban Environment

Homicides most frequently occur in the nation's larger central cities. In 1975,
25 percent of the nation's more than 20,000 homicides occurred in only ten
cities. Thus the rapid increase in the magnitude of the problem has been associated with an upsurge in homicide in a few selected places, mostly of the larger
and older central cities in the nation. Although the major increases are notable
in only a few locations, the risk of victimization has sharply increased in each
of the nation's fifty largest cities in less than a decade.[2] Yet there remains a
sizable gap in the risk of victimization among the nation's larger cities. However, only one of the ten largest cities possessed a victimization rate of less than
twenty per 100,000 in 1971-72, at which time both Detroit and Cleveland were
approaching homicide rates of forty per 100,000.[3] Between 1970 and 1973 the
actual number of homicides in the nation's twenty largest cities increased in all
but three places, according to a report by Klebba.[4] Cities, it seems, tend to
generate conditions which lead individuals, with increased frequency, to take the
lives of others.

### Homicide and City Size

Throughout most of this century the homicide rate in cities has exceeded those
in other political subdivisions. Homicide rates have been observed to increase as
a function of city size.[5] But large central city populations have been declining
for more than two decades, yet the homicide rates have shown a major upward
shift under conditions of population decline. Obviously support for an increase
in violent crimes based on opportunity, as a function of increased population
size, is not without its weaknesses.

### Regional Differences in Levels of Lethal Violence

It is clear from a review of the historical data that southern cities have shown a
propensity for a greater frequency of acts of lethal violence than have their
nonsouthern urban counterparts. However, urban regional differences have
diminished over time. By 1970, among the largest cities in the country, southern

cities were no longer totally dominant as environmental contexts in which the propensity for lethal violence could be demonstrated. Detroit, Cleveland, St. Louis, and Newark could now share top billing with Atlanta, Baltimore, and Washington. Does this shift in high homicide rates to nonsouthern environments lend support to Gastil's assumption that "with the mingling of American population through internal migration, the Southern tendency to violence has diffused broadly . . ."?[6] While Gastil's notion of a regional culture of violence has been questioned by a number of scholars, in terms of its validity, it is nevertheless an interesting point that we are currently unable to refute or support. However, Lundsgaarde's essay in this volume does demonstrate how cultural sanctions operate to lend support, negative and positive, to certain forms of behavior which lead to the commission of acts of lethal violence.

## The Question of the Role of the Urban Environmental Context on Lethality

The specific attributes of the urban environmental context impinging upon the propensity for lethal violence are seldom explored. But just as there are major variations in homicide rates among urban places, there are also major variations in local environments of occurrence. To be sure, high-risk environments tend to have specific locations within an urban context. A recent assessment of homicide patterns in Chicago verifies that most homicides in that city are confined to very few neighborhoods in selected zones of the city. To date one is unable to determine if high homicide risk environments remain relatively stable or fluctuate, within some general sector of the city, from year to year. Our understanding of this facet of the homicide syndrome is least understood.

Unfortunately the role of the environment remains unclear, and the essays in this volume do not go far in illuminating our understanding. The importance of the total environmental complex on behavior that terminates in the commission of acts of violence was cited recently by an individual who was engulfed in a life of criminal violence for most of his thirty-five years. John Allen starts his autobiography *Assault With A Deadly Weapon* with the following comment: "It seems to me that the kind of neighborhood you come up in may make all the difference in which way you go and where you end up."[7] For some forms of lethal violence a physical orientation which leads to more effective design measures may represent an appropriate goal, but in order to more fully comprehend the total context of all forms of lethal violence one should examine the role of the environment in greater detail.

## Participants in the Act of Lethal Violence

The population most often caught up in acts of lethal violence are those persons on the lower end of the income spectrum. A cursory examination of the death certificates of homicide victims often shows the individual to be described as a laborer and in many instances as unemployed. A review of the record of life-time earnings of a sample of persons killed in St. Louis in 1973 reveals a paucity of earned income. This limited income is both a reflection of being engaged in low-paid occupations and being unemployed at sometime during a given year. The same kind of information is less readily available for offenders, but there is no reason to suppose that the status of the offender is higher than that of the victim. The victim and offender are generally thought to possess equivalent social status. However, this might be changing as a result of the increase in robbery-motivated homicides.

### The Question of the Impact of Social Status on the Propensity for Violence

There are those who contend that poverty heightens the possibility for the use of violence in conflict situations. It has been said that the child rearing practices of poor families incorporate techniques designed to foster aggression as a method of self-defense. Piuck notes that the basic child-rearing rules employed by low-income parents to regulate behavior can have an inhibitory effect on ego development when applied intensely.[8] The latter writer believes that these child-rearing practices, which include physical punishment, can lead to a lessen-ing of the internalization of guilt and the promotion of aggression, with little provocation, toward persons who are not feared. Piuck comments: "Today black children and most poor children find external society less threatening than their parents."[9]

Child-rearing practices have also been discussed by Gold. He contends that the more common practice of physical punishment of children by lower-class parents leads to the likelihood of greater externalization of aggression.[10] Thus, the propensity for homicide is assumed to be greater among the lower class, while suicide is assumed to be more frequently associated with persons reared in a middle-class social milieu. Others have approached the direction and/or target of aggression in terms of role theory. Palmer hypothesizes the greater propensity for homicide to be associated with segments of the population characterized by low levels of social integration in the larger society, with suicide representing a more common phenomenon among those characterized by a high level of social integration and subsequent role loss.[11] On the basis of Palmer's assessment one should anticipate the level of externally directed vio-lence to be higher in those urban environments where role unreciprocity and/or blockage is high.

Poverty areas and zones of working-class dominance frequently emerge as high-risk homicide environments. In 1973, thirteen of Chicago's seventy-six Community Areas accounted for more than 50 percent of that city's homicide victims. Block notes that between 1971 and 1973, 2 percent of the blocks in Chicago were the sites of 22 percent of the homicides.[12]  In this same three-year period almost 1,200 persons were killed in these thirteen Community Areas, which constitute fewer than 20 percent of all of the city's Community Areas.

## The Role of Demographic Characteristics on the Changing Incidence of Violence

Homicide does not strike randomly, but selects, for whatever reason, those who are prone to engage in acts of externally directed violence. The risk of becoming a victim of homicide is heightened if one is male, black, and youthful. While the risk of homicide victimization has increased in the general population since the early 1960s, the highest risk continues to be associated with the previous set of demographic characteristics. There are those who contend that the recent rise in homicide simply represents the coming of age of the post-World War II baby-boom population.

Barnett and others do not grant the latter explanation much plausibility, since only 10 percent of the increased incidence of homicide can be explained by simple age structure changes.[13]  Block found that demographic shifts accounted for only 11 percent of the increase in homicides in Chicago during a recent ten-year period. It is true that demographic shifts explain only a small part of the approximately 85 percent increase in homicide levels occurring between 1960-61 and 1970-71;[14] nevertheless we should be aware of the contribution of the most vulnerable age groups to the total violence syndrome. During the above period the most rapid rate of change occurred among the 15-24 age group.

There was almost a doubling of the homicide rate among this age group during the 1960s. Klebba indicates that the 15-29 age group in 1973 "accounted for 40.1 percent of all of the victims and 59.3 percent of all of those arrested for homicide."[15]  But, needless to say, the demographic shift is generally thought to be less significant than changing life-styles, attitudes, and values adopted by segments of our more youthful population. Waldron and Eyer attribute the increasing level of homicides of the 15-24 age group to increased alcohol consumption, impulsive rage, and a breakdown in respect for societal values.[16] Earls, a child psychiatrist, provides within this volume a more detailed assessment of the behavioral changes of youth and the potential impact of these changes on the propensity for violence. His assessment goes beyond what has generally appeared in the literature to date.

Homicide is one of the five major causes of early death;[17] the others are cardiovascular disease, cancer, infant mortality, and accidents. Among nonwhites homicide represents the number-one cause of early death. This situation is further highlighted by Lee and associates, who state: "Since homicide is likely to occur at a relatively young age, the number of potential years of life lost are far greater than those lost by an older person who succumbs to cancer."[18]  The latter issue is given an exhaustive treatment in this volume in the essay by Dennis.


*Sex Roles and the Propensity for Violence*

There seems to be little doubt regarding the strength and stability of the perceived appropriateness of sex roles on the propensity for behavior leading to homicidal death.  In 1973, 15,840 (77.4 percent) of the 20,465 homicide victims were male, and an even larger percentage of offenders were male.  Males are extremely disadvantaged by adopting life-styles that are high risk in terms of increasing the probability of death resulting from homicide.  Since family homicides account for only about 25 percent of all homicides, this increases the probability that most other homicides will occur between males.  These interactions frequently revolve around insults, minor debts, and jealousy.  However, the most rapidly developing pattern of interaction is associated with robbery homicide, most often a male-on-male phenomenon.  This latter pattern of interaction is treated extensively by Zimring.

Male predominance in interactions leading to homicide is likely to continue, but there is some evidence of renewed interest in the changing involvement of women in acts of lethal violence as both offenders and victims.  At present most of this interest seems to be centered around the battered-wife syndrome.  Given the increased use of guns in domestic altercations and the greater intensity of violence which often ensues in these situations, one might logically expect an increase in the incidence of female victimization.  However, white women are safer from the possibility of homicide than any other sex-color group in the country.

In this period of blurring sex-role distinctions, not only are women more likely to be victimized, they are also more likely to assume the role of offender in homicidal events.  Our attention is drawn to this phenomenon by the sensationalism of selected press accounts of battered wives who kill oppressive husbands.  While the increase in female participation in the homicide act is beginning to attract attention, there is still little information available to validate the notion that new cultural forms are emerging.  The implication, though, is that emerging cultural forms are supportive of female personalities whose involvement in acts of lethal violence is not likely to be severely constrained, as in the past, on the grounds that violent behavior is nonfeminine.  A recent assessment of the assaultive tendencies of a sample of female prisoners demonstrated that the assaultive group possessed many of the same psychodynamic traits as assaultive males.[19]

*Race as a Contributing Factor to*
*Increased Levels of Lethality*

The final demographic variable to be investigated in terms of its association with the incidence of homicide is race, Most official sources of homicide information report only sketchy information on differences by race in levels of homicidal victimizations at scales other than the national scale. At the national scale black victimization levels exceed that of the white population by a ratio of approximately eight to one. Given that the former group accounts for only 11 percent of the nation's population, it was the source of slightly more than 51 percent of all victimizations in 1973. The homicide rate for both racial groups has shown an increase during the most recent upsurge in levels of victimization. The rate of white increase has occurred more rapidly than the rate of black increase, but the difference in base level between the two groups continues to be extremely large. In 1973 the age-adjusted homicide rate for whites was 5.7 per 100,000, while that for all other races (primarily black) was 44.4 per 100,000.[20] This represents more than a 100 percent increase in white rates in slightly less than a generation, but a smaller rate of change for others. The gap between the races becomes even more pronounced when each population is disaggregated by sex, as black males represent the sex-color group most likely to be both victims and offenders.

There exists no other major killer of the American population that differentiates so intensely, on the basis of race, as does homicide. Vaupel illustrates that nonwhites are 8.9 times more likely to succumb to an early death by homicidal victimization than are whites.[21] This likelihood estimate exceeds that of hypertension, nutritional deficiencies, and infant mortality, all of which are generally used as a basis for distinguishing between the health care availability and vulnerability to individual diseases on the basis of race.

Male blacks constitute the single highest homicide group in the nation. This group has historically been a primary victim and offender. In 1972, other male (primarily black) victimization levels were estimated to be in excess of 80 per 100,000, the highest level attained since 1950. The situation of this segment of the population has become increasingly dire, and/or the ability to cope with both internal and external forces has become so burdensome that violent acting out, leading to death, has emerged as an adaptive mechanism. Our lack of understanding of what has become the fifth-ranking killer of all black males and the ranking killer of those 15-24 bodes ill for the scientific community. It was recently noted that our various theories relating to violent aggression do not enable us, with any reasonable level of confidence, to identify those persons who are likely to engage in acts of violence without understanding the environmental context in which individuals are likely to find themselves. Halleck specifically states: "The psychodynamics of violence must be understood in terms of the manner in which given individuals adapt to varying environmental situations."[22] While biological and cultural variables are obviously at work in prompting these outcomes, we are as yet uncertain as to how they function to promote hostile acts in specific situations within a given environmental setting.

Black contributions to homicidal death totals have been high throughout the period in which death registration data have been available. An examination of the racial character of homicidal deaths during the decade of the 1920s revealed that during that period black homicide rates were seven times those of the white population.[23] But even then the highest levels of homicide among blacks occurred in the cities. Even during this early period, cities such as Miami, Detroit, Cleveland, Atlanta, Chicago, and Birmingham possessed black homicide rates in excess of 100 per 100,000. Yet there were other large cities whose rates were less than the national black rate of thirty-seven per 100,000. These low-risk victimization cities included St. Louis, Washington, Newark, San Francisco, and Richmond. There is no obvious explanation for these differences. However, while the aggregate homicide rate for blacks is slightly higher currently, the high homicide city levels have tended to diminish.

The issue of the black-white differential in homicide levels is explained variously. There are those who contend that the higher propensity for violence on the part of blacks is an inherent biological trait, yet there is no scientific evidence to support this position. Likewise it has been suggested that cultural differences possibly play a role in promoting the differential incidence. In discussing the environment in which large numbers of urban black children are socialized, Heacock states the following:

> Black slum child[ren are] also constantly exposed to death. Killer fires that take the lives of neighbors and friends, overdoses, drugs, gunfights and knife fights, and neonatal deaths from lead poisoning and infection all contribute to the high slum mortality rate. In short, for these children the world is truly a life-threatening place.[24]

This position, it seems, would provide some support for the notion of the evolution of a subculture of violence, as it is through violence that one learns to effectively negotiate one's environment. Wolfgang favors the notion that the subculture of violence is culturally transmitted from generation to generation.[25]

Another explanation for these differences no doubt finds greater support in the area of differential access to rewards, incongruence in social status, group-specific coping behaviors, and unique situational paradigms. Yet there is evidence of psychological impairment in numerous instances. It has been reported that in one city in the East, black offenders are frequently labeled "normal primitives" by diagnosticians of the court clinic who prepare a presentence evaluation for the judge.[26] The normal-primitive classification implies that one is free of mental illness and is behaving normally within the context of one's culture. If such practices are widespread a larger proportion of black homicidal offenders may indeed be mentally impaired. Herjanic reported that 15 percent of the 1973 homicide victims in St. Louis had previously been diagnosed as suffering psychiatric impairment.[27]

A final note on racial differences in the incidence of homicide is drawn from prison populations. In 1973, the number of prison homicides for which the race of the victim was known was 112. Fifty-six percent of the victims were white, while 54 percent of the prisoners were white. Interracial homicides in prison settings constituted a small percentage of the total, a pattern which corresponded to that prevailing in the larger society. This situation led the authors to conclude the following: "It is possible that an explanation for this lies in the fact that the socio-cultural factors which create the discrepancies in the homicide victimization rates of the two racial groups in the general population are ameliorated by conditions of prison life."[28] The implication is that when groups are confined to environments of great similarity, the differences assumed to be race related are minimized. Apparently the kind of urban social world in which blacks and whites participate is so different that life becomes increasingly cheap in the former, while highly valued in the latter.

## Changing Victim-Offender Relations

Several essays in this volume observe both the existing and changing relationship between victim and offender. It is the complex nature of this relationship that has fostered a general unwillingness on the part of the appropriate public agencies to attempt to intervene in interactions which often lead to a homicidal outcome. Perhaps the most incisive work in this area is represented by Wolfgang's *Patterns in Criminal Homicide.* But that work was confined to a single city and describes patterns that might have been considered typical more than a generation ago. However, a number of scholars have attempted to replicate Wolfgang's findings using more recent data from other cities. The work of Zimring in this volume appears to grow out of the latter tradition, but tends to emphasize the changes in victim-offender relationships over time. Other essays in this volume only indirectly focus on victim-offender relationships, but nevertheless provide insight into this primary element of homicidal behavior.

### The Changing Nature of Interpersonal Relations and the Commission of Acts of Lethal Violence

The nature and intensity of interpersonal relationships are thought to be altered by residence in large urban environments. It has been said by some social commentators that the American family structure is weakening, leading to a breakdown in traditional values; that low-intensity interactions create more widespread feelings of impersonalization; and that the increased desire to acquire material goods often transcends the need for respect when interacting with others. No doubt these changes have impacted upon the growing level of violence in American society in general and within specific environmental contexts in particular. The crux of the problem of increasing levels of lethal violence revolves around how people relate to people in a specific psychosocial context and their ability to render physical harm to others when conflict situations arise. Zimring, a contributor to this volume and an advocate of a policy to limit the availability of handguns, supports the latter effort as a means of minimizing the level of lethal violence. However, others who support the right of citizens to bear arms think that such a strategy would have little impact. It seems apparent, though, that effort must be aimed at altering the psychosocial dynamics of interpersonal relations as well as treating the problem in a mechanistic way, as much deterrent policy appears to do.

Most acts of homicide continue to be committed by persons known to one another. In 1970-71 approximately 40 percent of all homicidal deaths occurred as a result of violent altercations between acquaintances. These violent acts are generally thought to ensue as a result of some trivial action, heightened to levels of importance as a result of alcoholic consumption. Another 25 percent were associated with conflict within the family. In the latter situation husband-wife killings account for about one-half of the total. The enormity of the latter is beginning to attract the interest of agencies that are attempting to design deterrent-oriented programs. The major growth pole in homicidal patterns is that associated with felony-related crimes. By 1970-71 felony-related homicides accounted for nearly 30 percent of the total.

Different societal attitudes relating to homicide are found to correspond to the circumstances under which the act occurs and to the relationship between the victim and offender. Lundsgaarde illustrates the importance of the former element in his essay which follows. It is clear that when some specific social norms are breached public attitudes may support either the victim or the offender, depending upon which individual was considered guilty of committing the breach. Lundsgaarde hypothesizes that the severity of punishment in homicide cases is a function of whether the act falls within the private or public domain.[29] He further demonstrates the court response to differences in the homicidal setting by illustrating that only about 50 percent of the suspects cleared in 1969 Houston cases received negative sanctions.[30] The circumstances in about 40 percent of the cases were such that the offender was not severely punished, an indication that the nature of the circumstances led to culturally sanctioning the act.

*Felony Homicides: The Primary Focus of Public Attention*

The sharp increase in the number of felony-related homicides since the middle 1960s has attracted national attention. In 1960 only about one-fifth of all homicides involved felony murders, but by 1970 the percentage had increased to almost 30 percent. Regional differences exist in terms of the contribution of the latter homicide type to the total. During 1974, only about 20 percent of all homicides in the South were known or suspected felony types, whereas approximately one-third of the homicides in the non-South fell into this category. This in part is associated with the presence of more numerous large cities in the non-South than in the South. Preliminary evidence also indicates that victim-offender relationships vary substantially among that group of cities that might presently be described as high homicide rate cities. During the early 1970s the number of victims who were unacquainted with the offender or the offender was unknown was substantially higher in Detroit than in Atlanta. The homicide clearance rate declines as the number of stranger homicide victimizations increases. The lowest homicide clearance rates in 1975, in the nation's eleven largest cities, occurred in Los Angeles (65 percent) and New York (64.5 percent). Nationally in the same year 78 percent of all homicides were cleared. In 1969 the national clearance rate was 86 percent.[31] The decline in the national homicide clearance rate might serve as an indicator of the growing importance of felony murders.

*Family Homicides and Crisis Intervention*

There is an expression of growing concern regarding the seriousness surrounding levels of family homicides. Wolfgang notes the caveats frequently expressed by the police, indicating the danger associated with attempts to intervene in family conflicts.[32] These caveats will become less valid as programs to prepare police for this task are developed. Boudouris is also of the opinion that programs can be designed which can assist in lowering homicide rates in cities.[33] He indicates that New York City's program on family crisis intervention, however, did not show evidence of reducing homicide rates.[34]

In 1973, the Kansas City Police Department was awarded a grant to study the relationship between domestic disturbances and violent crimes. This group found that the best predictors of domestic violence were: 1) the presence of a gun; 2) a history of previous disturbances; and 3) the presence of alcohol.[35] Similarly, the Atlanta Police Department has been awarded a grant to develop a domestic crisis intervention team. The objective of this program is to reduce the number of homicides and aggravated assaults by 3 to 5 percent in the target area in which the crisis intervention team will be patrolling.

The promotion and development of domestic crisis intervention centers within police departments represent an innovation and a recognition of the seriousness of the problem of domestic violence. The many forces which are at work to set the stage for domestic violence must be confronted if we are expected to lower the homicide level among this specific segment within society. Most of the newly developed crisis intervention programs are too new to judge their effectiveness, but at least they offer a modicum of hope.

### Acquaintances and Levels of Lethal Violence

Little effort to date has been expended on attempts to diminish the level of homicide among the largest single segment of the homicide dyad, acquaintances. The circumstances surrounding this category of homicide are the most diverse of all. They occur under a wide variety of circumstances and within a full range of micro-environmental settings. Unlike the previous two categories they are not so easily dichotomized as street crimes (public spaces) or dwelling-unit crimes (private spaces). They include a large number of young black males who engage in violent conflict growing out of what appears to most people as trivial incidents.

The triviality of the incidents leading one person to take the life of another appears to bolster the promotion of such concepts as "nomal primitives." This is borne out by the following description: "Interaction among such individuals often occurs in bars where arguments readily result in aggressive encounters. Compelled to fight any challenger of his masculinity or courage, the 'normal primitive' protects himself by carrying a lethal weapon."[36] Notions of this sort simply provide a rationalization for overlooking the problem as a serious one because of its perceived intractability or the status assigned to the participants. Bruce-Briggs, in criticizing advocates of gun control, who are attempting to regulate the availability of the "Saturday Night Special," points out that neither side is very much concerned about this particular issue per se, but that this strategy was chosen because this particular weapon was cheap and was sold to a particular class of people.[37] He indicates that the name is sufficient evidence— the reference to "nigger-town saturday night."[38] A failure to foster positive self-identification among individuals, and to have that identification tied to the norms of the larger society, will continue to provide fuel for negative acts of aggression leading to an early demise. It seems that it is only when these acts of aggression are directed at members of other social status or racial groups do these persons receive societal attention.

The phenomena of intergroup-directed aggression is a complex issue and one which must be approached cautiously. Its difficulty, though, should not serve as a basis for retreating from the problem. But given the court psychologist's penchant for developing taxonomies (for example, "normal primitives") that simply lead to isolating aggressors from the larger society, rather than recommending treatment, then the lowering of the incidence of acts of lethal violence among acquaintances is not likely to be severely altered in the near future.

*Social and Psychological Support Services*
*for Dependents of Victims*

Many of the issues which are treated in this volume have received extensive attention by a wide variety of scholars.  The one issue which is only now beginning
to receive attention, at least in terms of homicidal death, is the services required
and available to the next of kin or spouses of the deceased.  Jackson provides us
with a review of the literature in this emerging field in the final essay in the
volume.  Because of the status of both the victims and the dependents it was
unlikely, until recently, that these persons could look forward to receiving
support beyond the family circle or the church.  But, in large urban environments
where it appears that the extended family is less functional and secularity pre-
dominates, are the traditional sources of support adequate to individuals through
these periods of crisis?  One would think that contact with nontraditional
sources of support would at times be necessary to assure that the distressed
individuals were returned to normal functioning without excessive delays.

It is becoming increasingly apparent that acts of lethal violence intensify
the level of stress in those communities where stressors appear to be ubiquitous.
In such stress-filled environments is it any wonder that acts of aggression leading
to more stress are commonplace?  Hopefully, the Mental Health Center movement will be able to partially assist in providing psychological support to those
individuals who have suffered object loss and are thus temporarily incapacitated
in the performance of their normal roles.  The inclusion of this topic in the
present volume is simply indicative of how important it is believed to be in terms
of promoting both individual and community health.  Bowlby in his discussion of
attachment theory says that the latter "is a way of conceptualizing the propensity
of human beings to make strong affectional bonds to particular others and of
explaining the many forms of emotional distress and personality disturbance,
including anxiety, anger, depression and emotional detachment, to which
unwilling separation and loss give rise."[39]  The point to be made here is that in
high-risk homicide environments the frequency with which affectional bonds
are broken is also high, and thus the expected level of stress can promote conditions of community paralysis, unless measures to intervene are available to
distressed parties.

## Summary and Conclusion

This volume attempts to present the current status of several facets of lethal
violence in urban America, where such violence tends to be concentrated.  Interest in this phenomenon is multidisciplinary, and thus contributors were

selected who represent the views and approaches to the problem which reflect both disciplinary bias and problem segmentation. The outcome for the reader, however, is hopefully a more holistic view of the complex nature of this issue. But we are painfully aware that a small volume such as this can only scratch the surface in attempting to state the case for the need to focus greater attention on an issue for which research into its many facets is sorely needed.

The growth in the incidence of lethal violence has increased several-fold since the beginning of the decade of the 1960s. This increase has been evident among all sex-color groups in the population. But it has reached crisis proportions among young black males, for whom it has come to represent the ranking killer. A national assessment of the cause and effect of this issue is in part related to how statistics are collected and subsequently publicized. While the FBI Annual Crime Report presents information showing the number of homicides by race and sex at the national level, there is no reporting of this kind of information for individual places. Similarly, the Center for Vital Statistics, which reports out all homicides (criminal and noncriminal), does not provide race and sex information for individual places. Thus the incidences of homicide among high-risk groups are masked by the aggregate rates describing the total population. An example of this masking effect can be discerned from 1970 Detroit data. In the latter year Detroit's homicide rate was estimated to be 34.5 per 100,000. When the population totals are disaggregated on the basis of race, one finds that blacks were characterized by levels of 66 per 100,000. Given the differential ratio of homicide between the sexes, the latter aggregate race-specific rate would no doubt reveal a significantly heightened male rate. Cleveland, whose aggregate rate has been similar to that of Detroit during the early 1970s, was reported to have averaged a nonwhite male rate of 142.1 per 100,000 during the period 1969-74.[40] Thus, the risk of black males succumbing to violent death tends to be unusually high in selected American cities, but that risk is submerged in the public data-reporting process.

Progress continues to be made in medical science toward a reduction in the incidence of all but the most intractable diseases. Even with the latter diseases there is continuous hope that a major research breakthrough will allow us to reduce their threat as well. A reduction in the incidence of automobile accidents is also having the effect of lessening the incidence of the primary behavioral cause of death. But the promise of lessening the risk of death resulting from acts of violence is less likely at this time. It is true that the total number of homicide deaths showed an absolute decrease between 1975 and 1976, but we are unable at this point to attribute this decrease to a random fluctuation, a change in age-sex-color specific risks, or to some of the intervention efforts introduced early in the decade.

It is hoped that this volume will focus renewed attention on the phenomenon that often escapes the attention of residents who have only limited contact with high-risk environments. Likewise, it is well known that behavior that has its origins in one environment often spills over into adjacent environments if efforts are not made to ameliorate conditions in the environment of origin. The growing interest on the part of social scientists in felony murder is simply an indication of the effect of the spillover phenomenon. But the total issue of lethal violence must be addressed by both the research community and service providers if progress is to be made in lessening the incidence of lethal violence.

## Notes

1. B. Bruce-Briggs, "The Great American Gun War," *Public Interest*, Fall 1976, p. 51.

2. Arnold Barnett, Daniel J. Kleitman, and Richard C. Larson, "On Urban Homicide; A Statistical Analysis," *Journal of Criminal Justice*, Vol. 3, 1975, pp. 90-91.

3. Ibid.

4. A. Joan Klebba, "Homicide Trends in the United States, 1900-74," *Public Health Reports*, Vol. 90, No. 3 (May-June 1975), p. 204.

5. Bruce H. Mayhew and Roger L. Levinger, "Size and the Density of Interaction in Human Aggregates," *American Journal of Sociology*, Vol. 82, No. 1 (1975), pp. 98-99.

6. Raymond D. Gastil, "Homicide and a Regional Culture of Violence," *American Sociological Review*, Vol. 36, June 1971, p. 414.

7. John Allen, *Assault with a Deadly Weapon, the Autobiography of a Street Criminal* (New York: Pantheon, 1977), p. 1.

8. Charlotte L. Piuck, "Child Rearing Patterns of Poverty," *American Journal of Psychotherapy*, Vol. 4, Oct. 19, 1975, p. 492.

9. Ibid., p. 496.

10. Martin Gold, "Suicide, Homicide, and the Socialization of Aggression," *American Journal of Sociology*, Vol. 63, 1958, pp. 654-655.

11. Stuart Palmer and John A. Humphrey, "Suicide and Homicide; A Test of a Role Theory of Destructive Behavior," *Omega*, Vol. 8, No. 1 (1977), pp. 48-50.

12. Richard Block, "Homicide in Chicago; A Nine-Year Study (1965-1973)," *Journal of Criminal Law and Criminology*, Vol. 66, No. 4 (1976), p. 510.

13. Barnett, "On Urban Homicide," p. 87.

14. "Homicide in the United States," *Metropolitan Life Statistical Bulletin*, Nov. 1974, p. 3.

15. Klebba, "Homicide Trends," p. 198.

16. Ingrid Waldron and Joseph Eyer, "Socio-Economic Causes of the Recent Rise in Death Rates for 15-24 yr.-olds," *Social Science and Medicine*, Vol. 9, July 1975, p. 387.

17. James W. Vaupel, "Early Death; An American Tragedy," *Law and Contemporary Problems*, Vol. X1, No. 4 (Autumn 1976), p. 73.

18. Yongsock Shin, Davor Jedlicka, and Everett S. Lee, "Homicide Among Blacks," *Phylon*, Vol. 38, No. 4 (Dec. 1977).

19. Alan R. Felthous and Bernard Yudowitz, "Approaching a Comparative Typology of Assaultive Female Offenders," *Psychiatry*, Vol. 40, August 1977, pp. 270-276.

20. Klebba, "Homicide Trends," p. 197.

21. Vaupel, "Early Death," p. 108.

22. Seymour L. Halleck, "Psychodynamic Aspects of Violence," *Bulletin of the American Academy of Psychiatry and Law*, Vol. 4, No. 4 (1976), p. 328.

23. H.C. Brearley, "The Negro and Homicide," *Social Forces*, Vol. 9, p. 1930.

24. Don R. Heacock, "The Black Slum Child and the Problem of Aggression," *American Journal of Psychoanalysis*, Vol. 36 1976, p. 328.

25. Marvin E. Wolfgang, "Family Violence and Criminal Behavior," *Bulletin of the American Academy of Psychiatry and Law*, Vol. 4, No. 4 (1976), p. 322.

26. Victoria L. Swigert and Ronald A. Farrell, "Normal Homicides and the Law," *American Sociological Review*, Vol. 42, February 1977, pp. 18-20.

27. Marijan Herjanic and David Meyer, "Psychiatric Illness in Homicide Victims," *American Journal of Psychiatry*, June 1976, p. 692.

28. Sawyer F. Sylvester et al., *Prison Homicide* (New York: Spectrum Publications, Inc., 1977), p. 15.

29. Henry P. Lundsgaarde, *Murder in Space City* (New York: Oxford University Press, 1977), p. 145.

30. Ibid.

31. *Uniform Crime Reports, 1974* (Washington, D.C.: U.S. Government Printing Office, 1974), p. 19.

32. Wolfgang, "Family Violence," p. 323.

33. James Boudouris, "Homicide and the Family," *Journal of Marriage and the Family*, November 1971, p. 675.

34. Ibid.

35. Domestic Violence and the Police, Police Foundation, Washington, D.C., 1977, pp. 26-27.

36. Swigert, "Normal Homicides," p. 19.

37. Bruce-Briggs, "The Great American Gun War," p. 50.

38. Ibid.

39. John Bowlby, "The Making and Breaking of Affectional Bonds," *British Journal of Psychiatry*, Vol. 130, 1977, p. 201.

40. Norman B. Rushforth et al., "Violent Death in a Metropolitan County," *New England Journal of Medicine*, Vol. 297, No. 10 (Sept. 8, 1977), p. 532.

# 2

# The Role of Homicide in Decreasing Life Expectancy

*Ruth E. Dennis*

## Introduction

The increasing trend of aggressiveness and violence in our society is reflected in the mortality and crime statistics. This is especially noted among groups such as nonwhite males, and youths of both races and sexes. Young nonwhite males are both victims and perpetrators of high levels of violence. In an earlier paper this author noted that the decline in life expectancy between 1960 and 1970 for nonwhite males was largely the result of the violent deaths of homicide, accidents, and suicides, respectively (Dennis, 1977).

Homicide is emphasized here since it is often associated with other forms of violence and social disorganization. The sensitiveness of this act to stressful events in the society makes it an easily observable indicator for social diagnosticians measuring social problems.

High homicide rates are preceded by socially predictable factors. Homicide generally shows its highest rates of occurrence in readily identifiable sociocultural variables, especially in the urban setting; for example, homicide shows a high correlation with unemployment, alcohol and drug abuse, prostitution, poor housing, high density, and so on.

The purpose of this discussion is to examine the role homicide played in the decreasing life expectancy of nonwhite males noted in the decade of the 1960s and to discuss some of the issues surrounding violence in this group.

## Mortality Trends

Prior to the mid-1950s, a downward trend in mortality rates was shown for both white and nonwhite males and females. Since that time, mortality rates for some age and sex groups have shown an increase. This reverse in mortality trends has been noted by the U.S. Public Health Service (1964). Some concern has been expressed about this unexpected turn of events. This trend reversal appears somewhat paradoxical considering the recent growth in the volume and scope of health services, including prevention, diagnosis, medical and surgical therapy, and rehabilitation. The improvement in the quality of these services, along with the availability of health insurance, making these high-quality health care services more readily accessible, should have further served to reduce or delay death.

Improvement of health care services was not the only factor operating to reduce mortality. Other factors noted were the rising standard of living resulting from improvements in work and home environments, the variety and quality of food, educational attainment, and recreational facilities. These data suggest that at no time in the history of this country have conditions appeared so favorable for health progress.

The above report further speculated as to the cause of this reversal, and examined the impact of radioactive fallout, air pollution, and other man-made hazards, recognizing the fact that death cannot be delayed indefinitely, but that, at some point in time, the mortality rate must level off as it reaches an irreducible minimum, or even increase as the population ages.

In attempting to examine the reasons for the change in mortality trend the Public Health Service examined mortality: 1) by state, looking for geographical variations; 2) by age; and 3) by cause of death or disease conditions. It was concluded that the change in mortality trend was the result of: 1) the leveling-off of the past successes in the prevention of death from infectious diseases; and 2) mortality from chronic diseases, accidents and other violence.

## Leading Causes of Death

The leading causes of death that have been mostly responsible for the observed trends in mortality rates vary slightly by race, and substantially by age. The overall leading killers continued to be heart disease, cancer, stroke, and accidents. However, violent deaths by accident, homicide, and suicide are the three leading killers of the young male. The increase in mortality rates for nonwhite males continued from about 1955 until about 1972 (see figure 2-1). The causes of death that are responsible for the increase in the overall mortality rates are increasing rates of accidents, homicide, and cirrhosis of the liver. Young nonwhite males are victims of homicide at a disproportionate rate (see figure 2-2). However, the overall homicide rate has shown a decline since 1973.

## Life Expectancy and Homicide

During the 1960s the life expectancy of whites of both sexes and nonwhite females increased, while the life expectancy of the nonwhite male decreased. In 1960, life expectancy in the United States was 74.1, 67.6, 66.5, and 61.5 for white females, white males, nonwhite females, and nonwhite males, respectively.

In 1970 the life expectancy had increased to 74.49, 67.94, and 69.05 for the white female, white male, and nonwhite female respectively, but had decreased to 60.98 for the nonwhite male (United States Life Tables, 1959-61 and 1969-71).

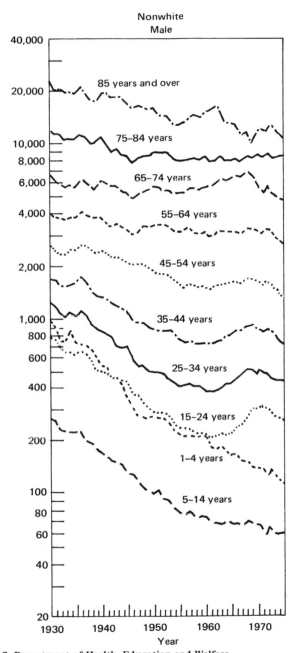

Source:  U.S. Department of Health, Education and Welfare.

**Figure 2-1.** Mortality Trends for Nonwhite Males, United States 1930-1975

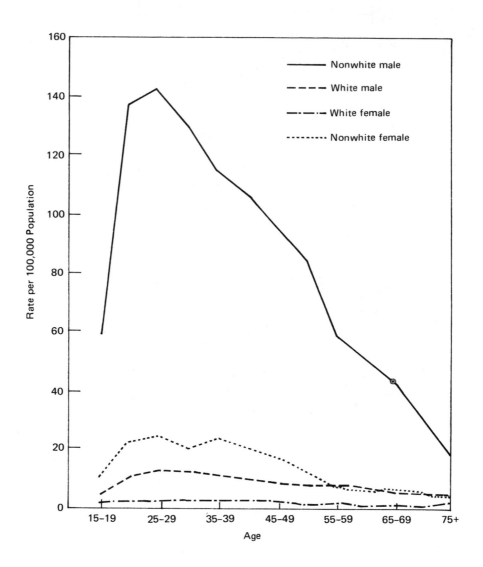

Source: Vital Statistics of the U.S., 1970.

**Figure 2-2.** Homicide Rates per 100,000 Population by Age, Sex, and Race, 1970

Thus, we find that the only group for which life expectancy has decreased during this period is the nonwhite male. It should be noted that we are using the United States Census definition for nonwhites which includes blacks, Native Americans and Asians. Since 1970 the life expectancy for all four groups has increased. In 1975 the life expectancy was 77.2, 72.3, 69.4, and 63.6 for white females, white males, nonwhite females, and nonwhite males, respectively.

Life tables show that while the life expectancy of both whites and non-whites increased substantially during this century the life expectancy gap between these groups has not been closed. The data showed further that there has been a narrowing of this gap for every decade up until 1960. In 1900 the life expectancy was 51.1, 48.2, 35.0, and 32.5 for white females, white males, nonwhite females, and nonwhite males, respectively. The difference between white and nonwhite female life expectancy was 16.1 years, and the difference between white and nonwhite males was 15.7 years. By 1975 this difference was 4.9 and 5.8 years for the white and nonwhite females and the white and nonwhite males, respectively. Expectation of life at birth has been higher for whites than for non-whites throughout the period in which records have been kept. Further, life expectancy for whites has been greater than that for nonwhites at all ages except for older ages (seventy years and over).

The higher mortality rates and resulting lower life expectancy, of course, affect the number of survivors, so that the number of survivors for each cohort is less for nonwhites than for whites. The difference in the number of survivors between whites and nonwhites is greatest between the ages of fifty and sixty. This difference reflects the higher death rates among young nonwhites. The decrease in the life expectancy of nonwhite males in the decade of the 1960s was probably more notable in urban areas with a high concentration of young nonwhites; for example, in Michigan the life expectancy decreased from 64.3 to 61.1 years during this period of time. This decrease in life expectancy assumes historical significance because it defies the long-term trend in increasing life expectancy of all major American population groups over the last century.

The significance of this decrease is far greater than the gross statistics might imply, since it was determined that the decrease was accounted for chiefly by young men who die violent deaths. Accidents, homicides, and suicides are the leading causes of deaths for males aged twenty to twenty-nine; however, young nonwhite males die at a rate of nearly twice that of young white males; the rate of increase for homicide was greater than any of the leading causes of death. The age-adjusted rate for homicide in 1960 for non-white males was 41.9, but almost doubled to 72.8 in 1970. Evidence suggests that the dramatic increase in homicide was greatly responsible for the decrease in life expectancy during the decade of the 1960s and remains mostly responsible for the present lower level of life expectancy for nonwhite males (see figure 2-3).

The probability of dying from a given cause of death is one measure of the

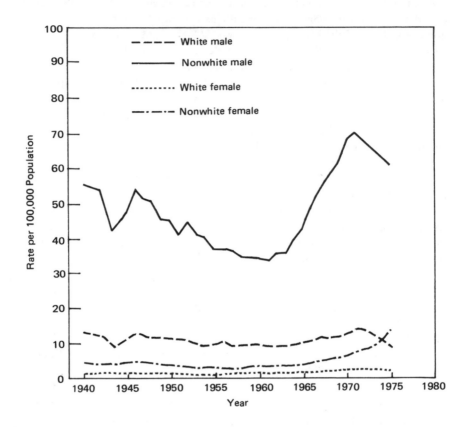

Source: U.S. Vital Statistics Reports, 1940-1975.

**Figure** 2-3. Homicide Rates by Color and Sex, United States, 1940-1975

importance of the various causes of death. Another measure is the gain in expectation of life that could be achieved if a specified cause of death were eliminated. When we compare the probabilities at birth of eventually dying from various causes, between the years 1951-61 and 1969-71, the probability at birth of eventually dying from homicide almost doubled from .02522 to .04527. The probability at birth of eventually dying from an accident (other than automobile) changed slightly, from .04024 to .04261. When we translate this into numbers, we find that, given the 1969-71 mortality rates, one of eight nonwhite males in Michigan ultimately will die from an accident or from a homicide. This probability compared with one out of seventeen for white males, one out of twenty-six for nonwhite females, and one out of thirty for white females (Kurt and Dennis, 1974).

Further, if we look at the effect in terms of the gain in expectation of life at birth resulting from the elimination of a specified cause of death, these calculations show that the elimination of homicide deaths would bring about an increase of approximately 1.4 years. Preston et al. (1972), in an earlier decade, found using 1950 vital statistics that the number of years of life gained since 1940 if violence were eliminated was 2.5 years. Since violent deaths have more than doubled since that time (about twenty-seven years ago) we could expect at least another year to be added at present if these causes were eliminated. This gain varies by place and group; for example, in Michigan we showed the gain in life expectancy from the elimination of homicide for nonwhite males to be 2.3 years between 1960 and 1970. This compared to 0.5 years for nonwhite females, 0.2 years for white males, and less than 0.5 years for white females (Kurt and Dennis, 1974).

The gain in the life expectancy for the nonwhite male, if homicide were eliminated, is greater than the gain from accidents or strokes. Yet the data are deceptive since most of the other leading causes of death affect older age groups, and hence have different ramifications than does violent death at an early age. Since violent deaths affect mostly the young, the years of life gained if these causes of death were eliminated or reduced may add up to a lifetime. Further, in the case of homicide it may add up to at least two lifetimes, that of the perpetrator and that of the victim.

## Some Implications of the Improvement in Mortality of the Young

The implications for a decrease in mortality rates for the young (say ages 15-34) obviously differ from those of older groups. The present emphasis for decreasing mortality rates is aimed at the leading killers—heart, cancer, and stroke. However, these deaths mostly affect older age groups, whereas violent deaths occur more frequently in younger age groups. A generally agreed-upon observation is that a decrease in mortality in the young generally is noted to affect the economy in terms of reduction in the loss of investments in higher education, work careers, and hence in the net per capita income. Further, decrease in mortality obviously affects families also; until only a few decades ago it was highly probable that one or both parents would die before their children reached maturity. For many nonwhite males the earlier state of affairs still exists; however, a significant reduction in deaths is likely to have the positive effects of increasing the survival rates of both parents and lowering widowhood, which would lower the number of female-headed households. All of these things may increase the likelihood of having more stable nonwhite families and change the male-female sex ratio at particular ages.

## Geographical Variations in Homicide and Other Violence

The evidence that homicide and other forms of violence affects life expectancy substantially has already been noted. In this section we will take a brief look at the geographic variations in the occurrence of violence.

It is known that homicide rates are higher in central cities than in the suburbs or rural areas. Klebba noted that, in 1970, 58 percent of the black population lived in central cities, compared with 28 percent of the white population. The homicide rates in the central cities were 85.4 and 8.8 for black and white males, respectively. Violence levels in central cities have been higher than in suburban areas or rural areas for as long as crime statistics have been recorded. The high homicide rates in central cities should be expected to reveal a substantial lower life expectancy for nonwhite males living there than for those living elsewhere.

Homicide rates also vary by region. The South has traditionally led the country in the incidence of homicide. While this trend still holds for whites, the North Central region now shows the highest homicide rates for nonwhites (see figure 2-4). This may be partially related to the large-scale migration of southern blacks into this region since World War II.

The geographical variations in homicide seems to correlate with the geographical variations in life expectancy; that is, the states with large urban areas showed the highest homicide rates and the greatest decline in life expectancy between 1960 and 1970. In the South, where homicide rates were traditionally high, life expectancy has been traditionally low. All southern states showed a decline in life expectancy, except Oklahoma.

Table 2-1 shows some of the variations in patterns of decrease and increase in life expectancy during the decade of the 1960s for selected states.

## Sociocultural Factors Linked to Homicide and Other Violence

There are numerous theories which attempt to explain the causes of violence and violent behavior. There have been suggested solutions for each suggested cause. Of course the most observable attempt to reduce levels of violence has been the incarceration of violent offenders in our penal system. The penal system has been accused of being ineffective in reducing violence because of its unfair and unjust policies, lack of programs for rehabilitation, too ambiguous penalties, lack of space, overworked personnel, and so on. Societal permissiveness, easy accessibility to handguns, drugs and alcohol addiction, lack of manpower, and

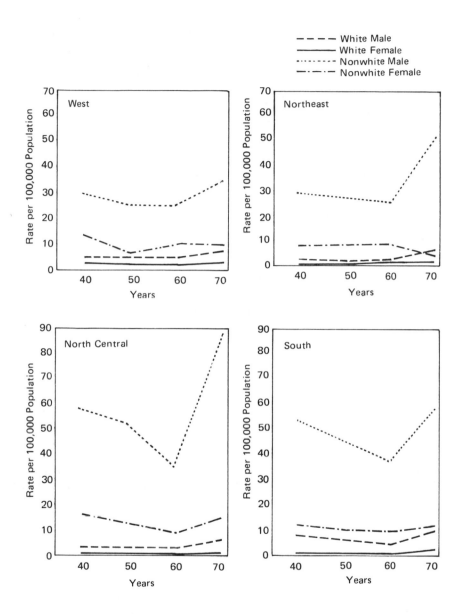

Source: U.S. Vital Statistics, 1970.

**Figure 2-4.** Homicide Rates for All Ages, Sex, and Race by Regions of the United States, 1940-1970

**Table 2-1**
**Life Expectancy 1960–1970**

| Decreasing | | Increasing | |
| --- | --- | --- | --- |
| *State* | *Years* | *State* | *Years* |
| Michigan | 3.30 | South Carolina | 1.06 |
| Pennsylvania | 2.25 | Hawaii | .99 |
| District of Columbia | 2.03 | Oklahoma | .55 |
| Illinois | 2.02 | | |
| New Jersey | 1.36 | | |
| Arkansas | 1.32 | | |
| Mississippi | 1.18 | | |
| Missouri | 1.17 | | |
| Florida | 1.06 | | |
| Ohio | 1.05 | | |

the payoff from crime also have been noted to be causes for increasing violence. Further, societal stresses resulting from poverty, ignorance, population density, poor health, inadequate food, unemployment deprivation and rejection, and so on are other sociocultural factors that have been linked to violence. A top official of the Tennessee Correction Department stated that the cumulative sociocultural stresses encountered by many black people (especially the poor) make them prime candidates for violence.

As we can see, reasons for violence and violent behavior are very complex and solutions will be difficult to design. Both the complexity of this problem and the difficulty in finding workable solutions have perplexed and confounded many concerned people (Sanders, 1974). Black people are especially appalled and bewildered by the state of violence in this country because they are the principal victims, and perpetrators. The FBI's Uniform Crime Report indicates that about 11 percent of the population of the United States is black, but about 27 percent of all reported crimes are committed by blacks. The ratio of *reported* crime is more than three times that for whites. More blacks than whites are arrested for serious crimes of violence, while whites are more likely to be arrested for crimes against property.

In spite of the complexity of violence and other crimes, social analysts should do more than just count the number of events. A major goal of any analysis of violence should aim to provide more insight into devising ways of reducing it.

The additional sociocultural stresses noted in the past two decades in most areas of this country have been associated with rapid social changes. Some of the most observable changes were:

1. Movement from rural to urban areas.
2. Movement from South to North.

3.  Changes in family structure.
4.  Economic and social changes.
5.  Political changes.
6.  Changes in communication and transportation (Dennis, 1977).

That a program concerned with the effects of rapid social change on the black population (especially) was not developed at the time of the 1954 school desegregation decision or even at some subsequent time when the major civil rights decisions were being made seems an indication of gross national neglect.

Castile (1975) speaks of an ethical responsibility of anthropologists to assist in suggesting ways in which a particular social goal may be achieved. At a meeting in Israel of the World Federation for Mental Health, the president of the federation, Louis Miller, stated that a major concern of the mental health professionals in Israel was how best to provide for the young generations, growing up in societies undergoing unprecedented rapid change (Miller, 1972). Castile notes that when rapid change in a subgroup is imminent it is the dominant group's obligation to assist in this change. He further states that

> if the pattern of changes is to be subjected to choice, it's these dominant societies that are in a position to most strongly assert control over these events.
>
> Directed change is obviously only successfully practiced by dominant societies, exercising some conception of what subordinate groups in contact with them should become. Both groups exercise choice, but choice for the subordinate group is frequently limited to acceptance or rejection of innovations introduced by the dominant group. (Castile, 1975)

Castile supports the theory of cultural pluralism for minority enclaves as a necessary condition for their *survival*. The "melting pot" theory which represents the antithesis of cultural pluralism needs to be reevaluated in terms of its possible long-term effect on community integrity.

Any discussion on homicide and life expectancy inevitably leads to how homicide, other violence, and crime are generally viewed. Homicide is not necessarily equated with crime here but it is synonymous with crime in most of the literature. Given that homicide is generally viewed as criminal behavior, then strategies for reducing crime generally should result in a lowered incidence of homicide. Darden distinguishes three points of view or schools of thought on strategies for reducing violence and crime:

1.  *The Conservative view (crime control) of crime*—Criminals should be treated as agents detrimental to the society regardless of the social forces that may have shaped their criminality. They represent a threat to others and should

be isolated until society can be guaranteed their future and good behavior. In this view recidivism argues for longer sentences and maximum-security institutions, while the solution for crime prevention is more police, more sophisticated equipment, and even the death penalty.

2. *The Liberal view (due process) of crime*—Liberals urge that civil liberties must be protected and that individuals cannot ultimately be blamed for many crimes resulting from socioeconomic factors. They believe we will not significantly reduce urban crime until we eliminate its principal social causes. This group believes the answer lies in more funds, talent, and time to produce the kind of research necessary to take more rational, informed action. They propose sensitizing the enforcement and judicial institutions.

3. *The Radical view of crime*—The radical perspective views crime as the inevitable consequence of the competitive and alienating institutions inherent in capitalist societies. This group worries, justifiably, about the proliferation of important anomalies: there is no uniform criminal code; laws are selectively enforced. Some convicts are punished by a simple slap on the wrist; others are ignored completely; still others are put away in limited-security country clubs for six months. In their view we must restructure institutions and society in order to eradicate violence and crime (Darden, 1974).

While these three individual categories contain legitimacy and certainly warrant worthwhile consideration, all three of these views, along with underlying cultural factors, must be considered in planning solutions to violence. By following this the approach to the solution of violence would be similar to the public health model for eradicating a communicable disease—that is, by treating the disease (violence) at its source, for example in an improved penal system, and preventing the disease (violence) by eliminating conditions that causes it—for example, sociocultural stresses and their ramifications.

## Summary and Conclusion

Declining mortality rates slowed down in some groups late in the 1950s. However, there was a notable increase in mortality rates for nonwhite males between the ages of fifteen and forty-four. The leading causes of death responsible for this increase in mortality for this group were accidents, homicide, suicide, and cirrhosis of the liver. The mortality rates for whites are less than they are for nonwhites at all ages except for older black males. The lower mortality rates for whites result in a higher life expectancy than for nonwhites.

The high and increasing homicide rates noted among nonwhites between 1960 and 1970 were suggested to be mostly responsible for the decrease in life expectancy observed during that time.

The population at highest risk of homicide is nonwhite males between the ages of fifteen and thirty-five. They are most likely to live in the central city of the North Central region of this country, or in the southern region of the country. Their assailant was probably an acquaintance, relative, or friend about their own age. Both the victim and the perpetrator are usually confronted with the social stresses of unemployment, migration, and so on. The victim often has a past history of aggressive behavior that could be detected as early as his elementary-school years, according to some preliminary results of a study of black males.

Homicide is epidemic in the nonwhite population and serves as an indicator to a host of other precipitant social problems such as assault, rape, robbery, drug and alcohol addictions, poverty, and so on.

These problems have been compounded for nonwhite males, especially during the past two decades, as an outgrowth of rapid sociocultural changes. These changes are thought to have promoted a state of cultural ambivalence and social disorganization.

Finally, institutional racism serves as a umbrella to any precursor to violence and homicide for the nonwhite male. Therefore solutions to violence and reductions of homicide in this group must involve simultaneously: 1) the elimination of institutional racism; 2) the recognition and promotion of cultural identity; 3) the changing of values and goals by both white and nonwhite population; and 4) more equal access to an improved quality of life for all.

## References

Ball-Rokeach, Sandra. Values and Violence: A Test of the Subculture of Violence Thesis, *American Sociological Review*, Vol. 38 (December 1973):736-49.

Berry, John W., and Annis, Robert C. Acculturative Stress: The Role of Ecology, Culture and Differentiation, *Journal of Cross-Culture Psychiatry*, 5, 4 (December 1974): 382-406.

Castile, George P. An Unethical Ethic: Self-Determination Conscience, *Human Organization*, Vol. 1 (Spring 1975): 35-40.

Darden, Joseph, et. al. The Nature and Causes of Violence and Crime in America: Strategies for Change, an unpublished paper presented at a workshop at the College of Urban Development, Michigan State University, March 2-3, 1975.

Dennis, R. Social Stress and Mortality in Young Black Males, *Phylon* 38 (September 1977): 315-328.

DeRosis, Helen A. Violence: Where Does It Begin? *Family Coordinator*, 20, 4 (October 1971): 355-406.

Gastil, Raymond D. Homicide and a Regional Culture of Violence, *American Journal of Community Psychology*, 1 (April-June 1973): 113-137.

Gorwitz, Kurt, and Dennis, Ruth E. On the Decrease in Black Male Life Expectancy. *Public Health Reports*, Vol. 91, No. 2 (March-April 1976): 141-146.

Goulet, L.R., and Balles, Paul B., eds. Life-Span, *Developmental Psychology: Research and Theory*, New York: 1970.

Grinker, Roy, and Spiegel, John. *Men Under Stress*. Philadelphia: University of Pittsburgh Press, 1945.

Gruman, Gerald J. *A History of Ideas About the Prolongation of Life*. Philadelphia: 1966.

Klebba, J. Homicide Trends in the United States 1900-1924, *Public Health Reports*, Vol. 90, No. 3 (May-June 1975): 195-200.

Knowles, L., and Prewitt, Kenneth, eds. *Institutional Racism in America*. New Jersey: Prentice-Hall, Inc., 1969.

Lambert, Edwin M. *Human Deviance, Social Problems and Social Control*. 1967.

Levi, L., ed. *Society, Stress and Disease: The Psychosocial Environment and Psychosomatic Diseases*. New York: Oxford University Press, 1971.

*Life Stress and Mental Health*. The Midtown Manhattan Study., No. 1, New York, 1962.

Metropolitan Life Insurance Company. *Mortality Differentials among Non-White Groups*. Statistical Bulletin, 55 (July 1974): 5-8.

Miller, Louis. *Mental Health in Rapid Social Change*. Jerusalem Academic Press, 1972.

Preston, Samuel H., et al. *Causes of Death: Life Tables for National Populations*. New York: 1972.

Roberts, E.E., and Askew, C., Jr. A Consideration of Mortality in Three Subcultures, *Health Service Reports*, 87, 3 (March 1972): 262-270.

Robins, Lee. Negro Homicide Victims—Who Will They Be? *Trans-actions* (June 1969): 15-19.

Sanders, L. Effective Control of Urban Crimes: Mission Impossible? *Crisis* (March 1974): 79-81.

Spicer, Edward, ed. *Perspectives in American Indian Cultural Change*. Chicago: 1961.

Spradley, James P., and Phillips, Mark. Culture and Stress: A Quantitative Analysis, *American Anthropologist*, 74, 3 (June 1972): 518-529.

Sulton, G.E., and Cornely, P.B. Assessing Mortality and Morbidity Disadvantages of the Black Population of the United States. *Social Biology*, 18, 4 (December 1971): 369-386.

Uniform Crime Reports.

Willie, Charles V., ed. *Racism and Mental Health*. Pittsburgh: University of Pittsburgh Press, 1974.

# 3

# Determinants of the Death Rate from Robbery: A Detroit Time Study

*Franklin E. Zimring*

Rates of criminal homicide in the United States, always high in comparison with other developed countries, have increased dramatically since the early 1960s. The aggregate U.S. homicide rate estimated by the FBI more than doubled during the period 1963-74, and homicide rates in major urban centers have increased even more substantially.[1] As the rate of homicide has increased, patterns of criminal homicide have also changed substantially.[2] National data and studies of individual cities show that while the majority of all killings are still committed by friends or acquaintances of the victim, a substantial and increasing proportion of the "new American homicide" is the outcome of robbery—an event where victim and offender are usually strangers.[3]

This essay reports a time series study of robbery killing in Detroit during the thirteen-year period of 1962-74. The Detroit case study is of special significance for two reasons. First, information on robbery rates by weapon was not available for most cities prior to 1974. Such data are available in Detroit, making it possible to explore the pattern of weapon-specific death rates over an extended period of time. Second, the increase in robbery killing in Detroit was substantial: the city's population fell between 1962 and 1974, yet the number of police-classified robbery-motive killings increased from fifteen to 155 per year. This nine-fold increase in death rate provides an important opportunity to study the determinants of death rates from robbery. The first section of this essay reports our analysis of the data on robbery and robbery killings. The second section addresses some tentative policy conclusions.

### Collecting the Data

Data collection for the Detroit time series analysis was relatively uncomplicated. Information on robberies by weapon used was retrieved from the archives of the Detroit Police Department for each of the thirteen years under study. Individual descriptions of each of the police-nominated robbery killings during the period were excerpted from Detroit police homicide files and forwarded to the Center for Studies in Criminal Justice for analysis. For each killing, data were collected on the lethal weapon, the age, race, and sex of the victims, and age, race, and sex of offenders where this information was available. The essential strategy of the analysis was to mesh data on the incidence of robbery and data on robbery killings to see what can be learned about determinants of death rates from robbery.

We begin the search for explaining Detroit's increase in robbery killings by asking whether, and to what extent, the increase in robbery homicide is a function of the increase in the number of robberies. Figure 3-1 sets forth the trends in robbery and robbery killing for the period under study.

During the period under study, the number of robberies increased from about 4,200 to slightly over 20,000; the number of robbery killings increased from fifteen to 155. There are two reasons why the increase in frequency of police-reported robberies is an insufficient explanation of the increase in death rate. First, a four-fold increase in robbery cannot, a priori, completely explain a nine-fold increase in robbery killing. Second, while the relationship between robbery and robbery killing trends is close through the period 1962 through 1970, the two trends diverge after 1971 in a fairly dramatic fashion. Part of the explanation for this divergence may be that a decreasing number of nonfatal robberies were reported to or by the police after 1970. Because victim survey data is not available over most of the study period, the precise impact of differential underreportage cannot be investigated.[4]

A necessary correlate of the fact that increased robbery volume does not account for the increased number of robbery deaths is that the death rate per 1,000 robberies in Detroit has been increasing since 1970, as seen in figure 3-2.

Figure 3-2 illustrates the close fit in robbery and robbery killing trends prior to 1971 by showing a fluctuating and essentially stable death rate per 1,000 robberies. The divergence after 1970 in the two trend patterns is reflected in the increase in the death rate per 1,000 reported robberies to a level in the 1973-74 period that is approximately double the earlier noted values.

There are two points to be made about the relationship between robbery volume and the death rate from robbery in Detroit. First, the increase in robbery volume alone accounts for less than half of the noted variance in robbery killing. We can confirm this by taking the 1962 death rate (3.57 per 1,000) and multiplying it by the 1974 volume of robberies (20,300); the result of this procedure is an estimated seventy-two robbery killings, less than half the 1974 total and a figure that represents 40 percent of the increase in deaths.

The second way of looking at the impact of robbery volume is also important: given that the death rate from robbery has risen, increases in robbery volume have a powerful effect on the number of robbery killings. Thus, if the volume of robbery had remained constant and the death rate from robbery had increased to its 1974 level (7.6 per 1,000), only twenty-eight robbery killings would have occurred, less than one-fifth of the actual number of 1974 killings. The explosive growth in robbery killing is thus a function of the increase in robbery-specific death rates interacting with increased robbery

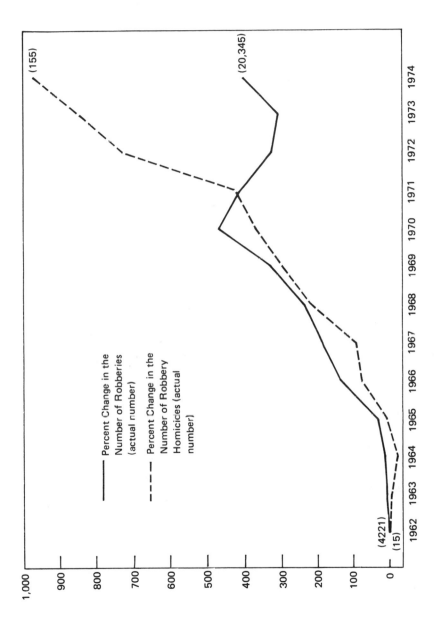

**Figure 3-1.** Trends in Robbery and Robbery Killing, Detroit, 1962-1974

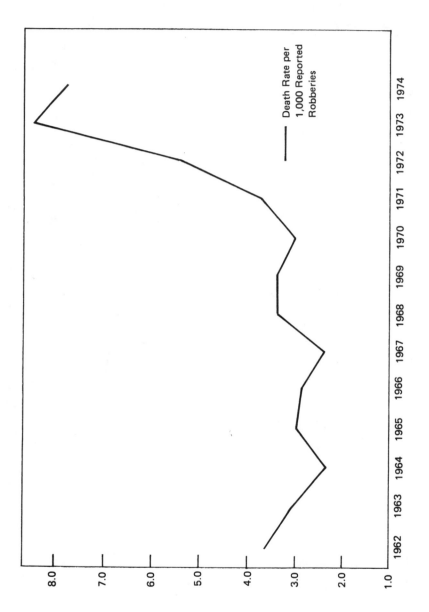

**Figure 3-2.** Death Rate per 1,000 Reported Robberies, Detroit, 1962-1974

volume. The remainder of this section attempts to explore this relationship further through a weapon-specific analysis of death rates and a somewhat more adventuresome correlational analysis of the relationship between weapon mix and death rate.

## Weapon Specific Death Rates

The availability and use of weapons can affect the death rate from robberies in at least three ways. First, if deadly weapons are selected for robberies, and an injury does occur, the use of more lethal instruments will increase the number of fatal injuries. The plausibility of this hypothesis can be illustrated by the fact that guns accounted for 72 percent of all robbery killings in 1974, but for only 42 percent of all robberies reported by the police. A second possible "weapon" effect is that the availability of deadly weapons makes robbery relatively easy and thus increases the rate of robbery and the total death rate from robbery. A third possible weapon effect is that the availability of deadly weapons decreases victim resistance and thus decreases the number of resistance-motivated robbery killings. The time series method and data are not sufficiently rich to directly address all three hypotheses, but it provides interesting observations that may be relevant to each.

Table 3-1 sets out the trend in robbery by weapon for the years under study.

The data in table 3-1 include both fatal and nonfatal robberies. As the table shows, gun robbery increased nine-fold during the thirteen-year span, compared to less dramatic increases for other types of robbery. The impact of this shift in weapon type on death rate from robbery can be traced by determining the weapon-specific death rate from robbery over the study period. These data are provided in figures 3-3 through 3-6.

Death rates from gun robbery are consistently higher than those reported for other methods of attack. Gun robbery death rates also increase during the period. Death rates from knife robbery are also relatively high but far less stable in trend. Strong-arm robbery has a persistently low and unstable death rate, with no apparent trend. Death rates in the residual category of "other weapon" fluctuate wildly with most of the higher values in more recent years.

The data in figures 3-3 through 3-6 can be both used and questioned. Our first use of the data is to determine how much of the increase in robbery death rate can be explained as a function of the increase in robbery combined with the change in weapon pattern. The method used for this estimate is to multiply the 1974 incidence of each weapon-specific robbery rate by the 1962-63 death rate for that weapon type. The death rate for the beginning years is determined by averaging 1962 and 1963 to provide a more stable baseline death rate. The method predicts a 1974 total of eighty-one robbery deaths,

**Table 3-1**
**Robberies by Weapon, Detroit, 1962-1974**

| Weapon | Year | | | | | | | | | | | | | Percent Change 1962-1974 |
| | 1962 | 1963 | 1964 | 1965 | 1966 | 1967 | 1968 | 1969 | 1970 | 1971 | 1972 | 1973 | 1974 | |
|---|---|---|---|---|---|---|---|---|---|---|---|---|---|---|
| Gun | 836 | 956 | 897 | 1,131 | 2,299 | 2,965 | 4,281 | 6,140 | 9,227 | 8,230 | 7,155 | 6,873 | 8,755 | 947% |
| Knife | 846 | 865 | 858 | 1,123 | 1,745 | 2,146 | 2,214 | 2,693 | 3,050 | 2,646 | 2,310 | 2,061 | 2,532 | 199% |
| Other | 376 | 543 | 829 | 856 | 1,426 | 1,864 | 2,060 | 765 | 774 | 819 | 782 | 871 | 1,158 | 208% |
| Strong Arm | 2,162 | 2,258 | 2,166 | 2,404 | 3,657 | 5,024 | 5,262 | 7,864 | 10,046 | 9,125 | 7,007 | 6,574 | 7,896 | 265% |

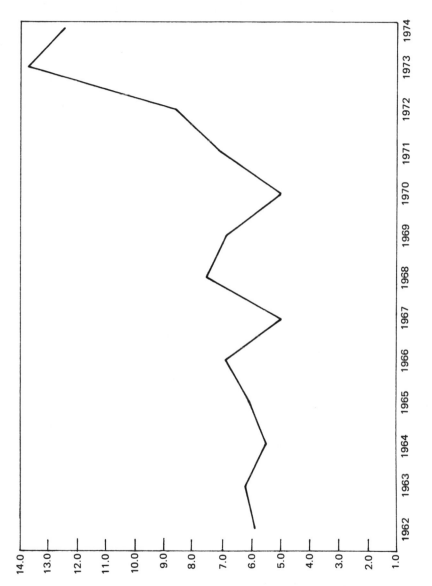

**Figure 3-3.** Trends in Death Rate per 1,000 Gun Robberies, Detroit, 1962–1974

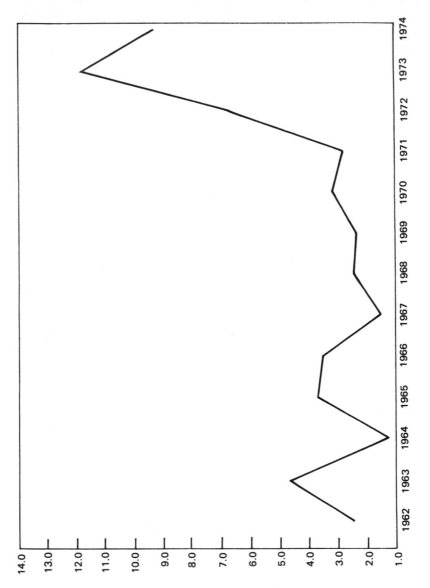

**Figure 3-4.** Trends in Death Rate per 1,000 Knife Robberies, Detroit, 1962–1974

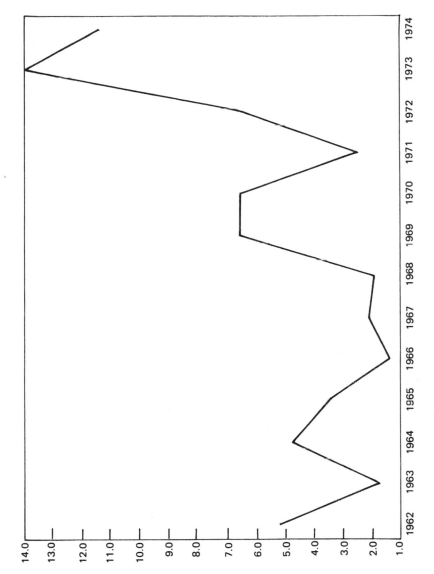

**Figure 3-5.** Trends in Death Rate per 1,000 "Other Weapon" Robberies, Detroit, 1962-1974

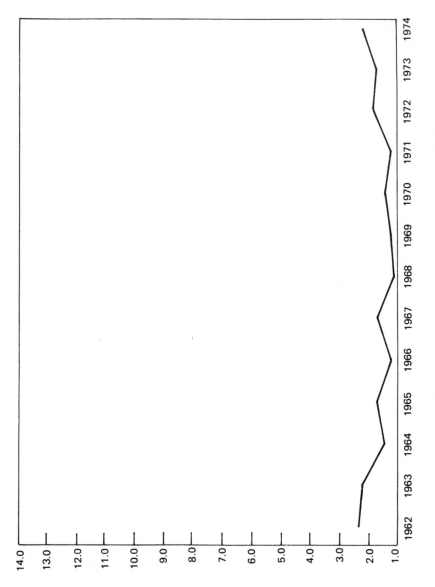

**Figure 3-6.** Trends in Death Rate per 1,000 Strong-Arm Robberies, Detroit, 1962-1974

slightly over half of the actual 1974 total and 47 percent of the increase in robbery killings. The remaining 53 percent of the increase in robbery killing is a function of the increase in weapon-specific death rates derived from police statistics.

The use of police-reported robbery rates raises serious problems in data interpretation.[5] To the extent that nonreporting of robberies has been increasing over time, the increase in robbery death rates could be an artifact of the fact that the denominator of the death rate—weapon-specific robberies reported by the police—may be a diminishing fraction of total robberies. There is also the problem than, often, homicides are difficult to classify by motive. In 1974, for example, 173 killings (65 percent committed with firearms) were listed as "motive unknown" by the Detroit Police Department.[6] The estimate of death rate is, therefore, an inexact one.

One method of testing the extent to which weapon choice as opposed to other factors influences death rates is to ask whether the frequency of a particular weapon use in robbery predicts the death rate from that weapon. Table 3-2 reports the zero-order correlation between the number of robberies committed with each mode of weapon and the number of robbery killings attributable to that weapon in each year under study.

The relationship between total robberies and total deaths is strong during the period studied, but disaggregating by weapon type reveals that the most consistent relationship is between gun robbery rates and the level of firearm robbery killings. The smaller relationships between knife robberies and knife robbery killings suggest that reporting and death classification difficulties are not merely theoretical problems in interpreting these data.

### Estimating Differences in Weapon Dangerousness

The reported death rate from gun robbery is higher than that for other weapons, but not as substantially different as other data or the correlation between gun

**Table 3-2**
**Relationship between Frequency of Robbery and Number of Robbery Deaths by Weapon, Detroit, 1962-1974**

| Weapon | Correlation | Significance |
|--------|-------------|--------------|
| Gun | .86 | > .001 |
| Knife | .46 | Not Significant at > .05 |
| Other | .09 | Not Significant at > .05 |
| Strong Arm | .51 | Not Significant at > .05 |
| Total | .76 | > .01 |

use and total death rate would suggest.[7]  One reason for this finding may be
that gun robberies are more frequently reported.  Table 3-3 tests this hypothesis
by comparing police and victim survey robberies in Detroit by weapon for 1973,
a year where both data sets are available.

The sample of victim survey robberies is small, but the difference in weapon
use is too substantial to be attributed to chance and has been noted in other
cities.[8]  The impact of this apparent difference in reporting robbery by weapon
on estimating death rate differences is substantial.  Using police robbery statistics, guns are 1.34 times more deadly per 1,000 robberies than knives.  Using the
police data on deaths, and estimating the relative frequency of gun versus knife
robbery from the victim survey (six to four guns as opposed to the officially
reported three to one) the gun appears to be 2.73 times as dangerous when used
in an armed robbery.  The same correction techniques estimate gun robberies to
be 3.5 times as deadly as "other weapon" robberies and seventeen times as deadly
as strong-arm robbery.[9]

### A Correlational Approach to Robbery Rates

The preceding analysis can directly address only one of the three hypotheses
about the influence of gun availability on rates of robbery.  More speculative
methods of inquiry are needed to address the other two hypotheses with these
data.  Specifically, we can use the percentage of all robberies involving guns as
a measure of firearms availability for robbery and test it against rates of robbery
and robbery killing.  The first query is a supplemental method of estimating the
extent to which gun use influences the death rate from robbery:  the specific

**Table 3-3**
**Percentage of Police- and Victim-Reported Robbery by**
**Weapon Type, Detroit, 1972[a]**

| Weapon | Police[b] | Victim |
|--------|-----------|--------|
| Gun | 41.3 | 28.1 |
| Knife | 13.4 | 18.6 |
| Other | 4.5 | 8.0 |
| Strong Arm | 40.8 | 45.3 |

[a]Detroit interviewed between January and March 1973.

[b]Fatal robberies deleted to create comparability.

analysis is the relationship between the percentage of all robberies committed by guns and the death rate per 1,000 total robberies.

Over the period under study, the correlation between percent gun of total robbery and robbery death rates was .68,[10] suggesting a high relationship between total robbery death rates and the percentage of all robberies attributable to guns. An initial caution is warranted, however, relating to the strength of the relationship and the nature of the correlation. The period studied involved an almost uninterrupted increase in the percentage of robberies committed with firearms and in robbery deaths. Despite the fact that there is independent evidence implicating firearms as a predictor of death rates, the statistical association between percent of all robberies committed with firearms and robbery death rates is subject to question because there is no basis for controlling for the independent effect of the passage of time, and all that the passage of time may mean, in exploring the relationship. This problem is compounded by the possibility that the "percentage gun" measure over time reflects not only gun availability but also changing patterns of robbery-reporting to and by the police. Since victims and police are least likely to report less serious robberies, the percentage of robberies attributed to firearms in official statistics would tend to increase as the percentage of all robberies reported to the police decreases. If the percentage of robberies not reported increases as the volume of robbery increases, the correlation between relative gun use and robbery rate may reflect, in part, the relationship between robbery volume and the tendency to not report. Our inability to control for all of the changes in Detroit that are attributable to the passage of time is a chronic problem in correlational analysis, unless the other determinants of robbery rates can be identified and measured. So little is known about robbery, particularly during the period under study, that a more refined model seems unfeasible.

Notwithstanding the difficulties of correlational analysis, the relationship between the percentage of all robberies attributable to guns and total robbery rates is worthy of note. During the thirteen years observed, the relationship between percentage of total robberies attributable to guns and total robbery rates was .94,[11] a statistical finding so large that it is usually a hypothetical rather than real product of social science research. The correlation is consistent with the hypothesis that firearm availability and use increase rates of robbery.

The noted associations are strong enough to suggest that any tendency for increased firearm use to decrease victim resistance and thus death risk is overwhelmed by the larger impacts of increased firearm use. Again, I must caution the reader that the steady increase in both robbery rates and the percentage role of firearms renders us unable to disaggregate the effects of time from the effects of firearms use. However, the extraordinary relationship between firearm share and total robbery rate appears sufficient to support at least a tentative finding of causal connection.

**Race, Victimization, and Offensivity**

While most homicide is intraracial in character, the common perception of
robbery and robbery homicide is of an event that involves a black offender and
a white victim. In fact, recent studies establish that urban blacks run higher
risks than urban whites of being involved in robbery incidents.[12] The data we
have on robbery killings show an interesting temporal pattern. Figure 3-7
presents data on the racial concentration of the city of Detroit, robbery-killing
offenders, and robbery-killing victims. For purposes of economy in presentation, the graph shows by year the percentage of all residents, all first offenders,[13]
and all robbery killing victims who are black.

   In the early years of the study period, the interracial stereotype of robbery
killing is confirmed by the data. Over time, with a rather abrupt change in the
late 1960s, the stereotype is reversed. By 1970 the majority of all robbery-
killing victims are black, and the concentration reaches 64 percent in 1974. A
shift in the racial mix of the city's population accounts in part for this change
but cannot explain either the extent of racial concentration in the latter years
or the suddenness of the shift in pattern. Some of the pattern may reflect
changes in police classification in questionable cases. But since the point of
abrupt change is not correlated with any sudden shift in the upward trend of
robbery killing, these data may also speak about the extent to which riot-
induced psychological segregation was reflected in the increased concentration
of crime victimization within Detroit's black community.

**An Important Unanswered Question**

Before proceeding to a discussion of the possible policy significance of our findings, it is important to emphasize the central mystery of these data—the extremely
high death risk associated with robbery when compared to other crimes with
property motives. Using policy-reported gun robberies as the denominator,
slightly more than one out of 100 gun robbery encounters will produce a death.
Correcting for underreporting by using the victim survey estimates, the proportion would be approximately one in 150.[14] Studies using other methods suggest
that the robber's physical security is not at risk in anything near this proportion
of cases.[15] Killing the victim to eliminate witnesses seems counterproductive in
that clearance rates for robbery killings are higher than the general clearance
rate for robberies. If robbery were a totally instrumental crime, at the point of
victim resistance or refusal, the rational robber should desist and find another
victim. The high and apparently weapon-related death rate from robbery invites
speculation as to whether it is appropriate to consider the robbery event as solely
instrumental. This is a question that can only be speculatively addressed on the
existing data, but it deserves extensive further study.[16]

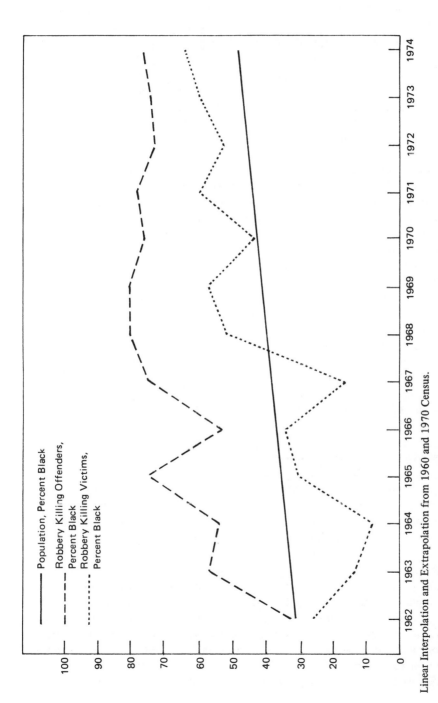

Linear Interpolation and Extrapolation from 1960 and 1970 Census.

**Figure 3-7.** Racial Concentration of Detroit Population, Robbery-Killing First Offenders, Robbery-Killing Victims, 1962-1974

The methods employed in this study are imperfect and must be supplemented with other research strategies. However, the tentative findings invite speculation about the implications of these data for research and public policy.

The weapon effects found in the present study are dramatic, yet prior studies of weapon effects are nonexistent. Robbery statistics were not even divided into weapon-specific categories until 1974 in the Uniform Crime Reports. When gun robbery is ten to seventeen times more likely to result in death than unarmed robbery, weapon-specific robbery rates are a necessary condition to minimally effective crime reporting.[17] Indeed, from the standpoint of death risk, the contrast between armed and unarmed robbery is as important as the contrast between unarmed robbery and other offenses. In the present study, as table 3-2 illustrates, a failure to introduce weapon-specific robbery data would have led observers to conclude that there is a strong and stable relationship between robbery volume and death risk, when no weapon-specific stability exists except for gun robbery. Such aggregation errors are probably common in the statistical study of crime, but no less regrettable because they are numerous.

The increases in weapon-specific death rates are difficult to interpret without longitudinal victim survey data. A substantial portion of the increase could be due to differences in reporting robbery over time, but it is unlikely that differential reporting tells the whole story because gun robbery is reported to the police in a majority of victim-reported robberies.[18] The sharp divergence between the stable gun death rates in the first phase (1962-70) of the study and the escalation of death rate in the second phase (1971-74) may also reflect changing patterns of victim resistance or offender intention. The historical data are not rich enough to address this important topic.

## Toward a Criminal Law of Robbery

The data are relevant to criminal law in at least three ways. First, they support the distinction made by criminal law both in theory and practice between armed and unarmed robbery. Second, these data call into question an indiscriminate scope of the felony murder rule. Third, they suggest that effective firearms control measures may affect both the frequency and lethality of robbery.

In penal policy, the distinction between armed and unarmed robbery should be crucial. Despite the fact that robbery without a weapon results in some injury more frequently than armed robbery, it seems apparent that no two behaviors that carry a death risk that varies by as much as a factor of seventeen belong in the same section of a rational penal code. Whether the relevant objective is marginal general deterrence or retribution, armed robbery presents a distinctive threat entitled to priority in the allocation of penal resources.

While the weapon used is an important element in grading nonlethal robbery,[19] any death from robbery, burglary, arson, and a small list of other offenses is typically treated as murder by common law and as first-degree murder by statute.[20] The common-law felony murder rule imputes "malice," the essential intent to do serious bodily harm needed to establish murder, from the intent to commit the felony whether or not any intention to hurt existed.[21] Since the robber who performs the lethal act is typically guilty of malice whether or not a felony murder rule exists, the practical significance of the rule is to generate liability for accomplices to felonies for the crime of murder whether or not they concurred in the lethal act.[22]

The logic behind the felony murder rule has encountered sustained and, in my view, successful criticism. If the rule is intended to deter inherently dangerous felonies, stricter penal treatment of all such inherently dangerous felonies is a more logical approach to that goal than a specialized rule for robberies with lethal outcome.[23] If, as argued by Justice Trainer of the California Supreme Court, "the purpose of the felony murder rule is to deter felons from killing negligently or accidentally by holding them strictly responsible for the killings they commit,"[24] it is ironic that the principal application of the rule is to generate liability not for the killer, but for his co-adventurers.[25]

Whatever the stated purpose of the rule, our preliminary data suggest that the long list of felonies usually included in the felony murder rule may, from the standpoint of penal policy, be self-defeating. If robbery deaths are substantially unplanned events, the different death rates observed in this study suggest that death is an accident that occurs far more frequently when the robber is armed. Removing unarmed robbery and burglary from the coverage of the common-law rule would, if any marginal deterrence operates, save lives unless the number of additional unarmed robberies produced by such a shift were ten times as great as the number of cases where the distinction in law persuaded the robber to leave his weapon at home.

The practical impact of any shift in felony murder coverage is difficult to predict and probably minimal. In contrast, any countermeasure that succeeded in reducing gun availability in robbery appears likely to reduce both the number of robberies and the death rate per 1,000 robberies. Reducing the number of robberies is an obvious social policy goal. Less obvious is the finding that reducing the level of weapon use in robbery can also have a dramatic effect on death risk. Moreover, it is more important from a public health standpoint to reduce gun availability when the rate of predatory crime is high. Detroit, like urban centers throughout the United States, has both a "gun problem" and a "crime problem," and each problem makes the other problem worse. The data from this study show high variability in both robbery rate and weapon mix; unfortunately, all the variation is in an undesirable direction. It is necessary to begin identifying public policy tools that can operate to produce downward variation of substantial proportions.

**Notes**

1. Compare Federal Bureau of Investigation, Uniform Crime Reports, 1963, at 3, 6-8, with Federal Bureau of Investigation, Uniform Crime Reports, 1973, at 6-10. See also Zimring, "Firearms and Federal Law: The Gun Control Act of 1968," *Journal of Legal Studies*, IV (1975): 133.

2. See Block and Zimring, "Homicide in Chicago, 1965-1970," 10 *Journal of Research in Crime and Delinquency,* 10 (1973): pp. 1, 7. See also Block, "Homicide in Chicago: A Nine Year Study (1965-1973)," *Journal of Criminal Law and Criminology,* 66, No. 4, at p. 496 (see especially pp. 505-509). 1976

3. See, for example, Block, "Homicide in Chicago." Parallel studies of Detroit and Atlanta have reported roughly similar findings.

4. The first national sample victim survey occurred in the field in 1966. The Census series of national and city level victim survey studies was initiated in 1972 and has, to date, reported at the city level in twenty-six cities. The 1966 National Opinion Research Center Study differed from the Census studies not only in the fact that it was a national sample, but in design and instrumentation. The census data available for Detroit victimization are based on field interviews conducted in 1973 and 1975, well into the time period under study.

5. See, generally, National Commission on Crime and the Administration of Criminal Justice, *The Challenge of Crime in a Free Society* (Washington, D.C., 1966), at Chap. 2.

6. The level of "motive unknown" killings has been increasing faster than the total homicide rate in Detroit and a number of other cities. The relative ease with which killings between close associates can be cleared by the police suggests that such killings are more likely to involve a victim and offender who are not closely related prior to the lethal act. The implications this has for the proportion of such killings that are robbery motivated are not obvious. Clearly, however, the margin of error in estimating robbery death rates grows more substantial as the number of unknown motive killings increases.

7. See the discussion accompanying note 9, below, and the correlational data reported at pp. 41-43, infra.

8. Preliminary data from a cross-sectional study of robbery in 1974 in sixteen cities indicate not only that victim reported robberies are a lower percentage gun than police reported robberies, but the correlation between the police reported percentage gun and victim reported percentage gun is a very modest .4. What this means, and which data set is appropriate for estimating the true incidence of robbery, is a substantive question that has not been successfully resolved.

9. Using victimization data, underreporting can be corrected but no specific death rate can be estimated. The data for "other weapon" robberies will be used as an example. The methodology is as follows:

Step 1. The deaths (reported by the Detroit Police Department) for "other weapon" robberies are expressed in terms of the percentage of "other weapon" and "gun" deaths (5/62 + 5 = 7.5 percent) for 1972.

Step 2. That percentage is then divided by the percentage that "other weapon" robberies represents of "other weapon" and "gun" robberies, (2291/7987 = 22.3 percent) estimated in the victimization survey (7.5/22.3 = .34).

Step 3. Steps 1 and 2 are repeated for "gun" deaths and robberies. The comparable "gun" percentages are found by subtracting the "other weapon" percentages from 100. The parallel gun percentages are 92.5 (100 − 7.5) and 77.7 (100 − 22.3). After dividing the former by the latter, which yields 1.19, steps 1 and 2 have been duplicated for "guns."

Step 4. The final ratios derived from gun and other weapon (1.19/.34 = 3.50) are the basis for estimating the degree to which guns are more lethal than "other weapons."

10. Significant at > .01.

11. Significant at > .001.

12. See Cook, "A Strategic Choice Analysis of Robbery," in Skogan, ed., *Sample Survey of the Victims of Crime* (Cambridge, Mass.: Ballinger, 1976), pp. 175-177.

13. Race data were collected for all robbery offenders but reported for the first offender only to control for the misleading racial characterization that results from any aggregation of total suspects or total arrests in violent crime. Younger offenders, particularly younger black offenders, tend to commit robberies in large groups. This fact, together with the younger age profile in urban black vs. white populations, means that counting all offenders will tend to overestimate the extent to which blacks are responsible for violent crimes. Methodologically, counting only the first offender's race assures that each robbery death has the same significance in the table, rather than making the importance of the lethal event turn on the number of offenders involved.

14. We have not been able to cross-tabulate, as yet, reporting propensity by individual weapon used in robbery. Chicago victimization data indicate that 58 percent of all robberies where a weapon was used are reported to the police. The persistently smaller percentage gun of total robbery in the victim surveys suggests that gun robberies are even more likely than other armed robberies to be reported to the police (see table 3-3 in the text). The figure reported in the text relies on an estimate that two-thirds of all gun robberies are reported to the police. There is a considerable margin of error in that estimate which awaits more specific cross-tabulation of the victim surveys and more sustained analysis of the reliability of the victim survey data.

15. Our study of 1,222 robberies in Chicago suggests a very modest risk to the robber's physical security. Moreover, the weapon-specific death rates in this study seem inconsistent with an "offender safety" theory of robbery killing: the more deadly the robber's weapon, the higher the probability that he will kill. Intuitively, the more deadly his weapon the greater the balance of terror

between offender and victim favors the offender. While this may be balanced off, in part, by heavily armed offenders selecting relatively harder targets for attack, one doubts that the balance is complete. In Detroit, sixteen citizens killed suspected robbery offenders, a rate one-tenth that of killing by robbery offenders. In an additional six cases, the police reported a justifiable killing.

16. To supplement the efforts reported in this time study, we are analyzing in detail a representative sample of robberies and robbery killings in Chicago during 1975, and attempting, cross-sectionally, to use police and victim survey data to explore the nature of the robbery outcome. Some of these data are reported by my colleague Richard Block in *Violent Crime* (Lexington Books, 1977). My own analysis of these data is still in progress.

17. Prior to 1974, the Uniform Crime Reporting Section would divide robberies reported by the police into armed and unarmed categories but place greater emphasis on the robbery category as a unit. Weapon-specific robbery rates were first collected on a one-time experimental basis about seven years ago by the Federal Bureau of Investigation and became standard reporting procedure in January 1974.

18. See, e.g., research reports cited in note 4.

19. See, for example, Illinois Rev. Stat. Ch. 38, § 18-1 and 18-2.

20. See, for example, California Penal Code, §§ 187, 189, 190, and 190.1; and Illinois Rev. Stat. Ch. 38, § 9-1(3).

21. See *People* v. *Washington*, 62 Cal. 2d 777, 44 Cal. Rptr. 442, 402 P. 2d 130.

22. *People* v. *Washington*, note 21 above, at 782.

23. See Holmes, *The Common Law*, p. 58.

24. *People* v. *Washington*, supra note 21 at 781.

25. For data on multiple offenders in robbery homicide, see Block and Zimring, "Homicide in Chicago," p. 7. See also Zimring, Eigen, and O'Malley, "Punishing Homicide in Philadelphia," *University of Chicago Law Review,* 227 (1976): 231-232.

# 4 The Social Reconstruction of Adolescence: Toward an Explanation for Increasing Rates of Violence in Youth

*Felton Earls*

Violence is a social problem, not a medical problem; it is fundamentally a response to economic inequities and only secondarily determined by personality factors. The opposite of the bald statement that violent behavior is a medical problem, caused by disordered minds, is no less provocative. Arguments for either position imply that the role of medicine is joined by concepts of the pathophysiology or psychopathology of individual violent acts. Society is likely to have a rather intolerant view of such polemics. Violence as a complexly determined public health menace appears to be escalating not only in frequency but in wantonness as well. Obviously, the solution to the problem will depend on the coordinated and mutually supportive roles of several social agencies and professions.

In this essay, I wish to explore the particular problem of violence among adolescents, since it is pivotal to understanding our current dilemma. I believe it is necessary to present a broad framework in which to understand the contemporary socialization of adolescents in American society for two reasons. First, it seems important to review what major concepts we have to aid our understanding of adolescence before applying what we know about this experience to the problem of violent behavior. Second, arriving too quickly at a narrow focus on a group of young people already known to have been involved in violent crimes necessarily constricts our attention to a clinical population which may or may not be different from other adolescents not involved, or not yet involved, in violence.

If we are to arrive at rational, far-sighted explanations for the increase in violence, we must know not just what specific social conditions or experiences encourage this behavior in some children, but in what broad and pervasive ways adolescence as a social experience is evolving in our society. I will refer to a general theme throughout this presentation: It is the special task of adolescents

Reprinted from *Perspectives in Biology and Medicine*, Vol. 22, No. 1 (Autumn 1978), with the permission of the University of Chicago Press. ©1978 The University of Chicago. This essay received honorable mention in the second *Perspectives* Writing Award for authors under thirty-five. An earlier version was presented at the Lethal Aspects of Urban Violence, Urban Research Center, University of Wisconsin, Milwaukee, Wisconsin, May 1977.

to examine and reconstruct the social order surrounding them. This is a result of the opening of new cognitive capacities at adolescence. The outcome of this effort will determine the extent to which the adolescent-turned-adult will contribute to the construction or destruction of his society.

I believe, with Berger and Luckman (1, p. 103), that "all societies are constructions in the face of chaos." The maintenance of the social order includes some tolerance for change and progress but always within a defined social, political, and economic context. Adolescents arrive at the stage of "operational logic" by examining various abstract, ideological concepts, such as those of nation, democracy, freedom, justice, etc. As these are reasoned through and examined for their reality content, the adolescent achieves a sense of personal and group identity, the result of which is social reconstruction. Short of revolutionary change, this adolescent dialectic results either in social progress or social decay.

Malcolm X, in his 1965 address to a group of Harlem youth, indicated his awareness of the constructive role played by adolescents:

> If you've studied the captives being caught by the American soldiers in South Vietnam, you'll find that these guerillas are young people. . . . Most are teenagers. It is the teenagers abroad, all over the world, who are actually involving themselves in the struggle to eliminate oppression and exploitation. . . . The young people are the ones who most quickly identify with the struggle and the necessity to eliminate evil conditions that exist. And here in this country it has been my observation that when you get into a conversation on racism . . . , you will find young people more incensed over it—they feel more filled with an urge to eliminate it. (2, p. 221)

I submit to you that it is the result of cognitive growth that adolescents feel urgency, become incensed, and act swiftly.

I think it is a consensus of opinion among those of us who devote at least part of our professional lives to the care and protection of adolescents that the social experience of adolescence is undergoing a degradation. Our focus on violence is justified, as the statistics reflect, because we are faced squarely with the fact that adolescents today are helping us to construct a society in which violence is a normative experience. Developing a perspective on adolescent violent crime particularly (because it represents a faster rate of increase than for other age groups) must be placed in a cognitive, emotional, and social context unique to this developmental period. When approached in this way, the experience of adolescence can be understood as an immature reflection of contemporary American society. Experiments with drugs, the sexual revolution, counterculture, the student protest movement, antiwar demonstrations, and accelerating violence, while made into public nuisances by adolescents, are their attempts over the past fifteen years to incorporate ideas and images from the world of adults into a process of social reconstruction to achieve a personal meaning.

Before discussing the various ways we have to explain why violence is becoming epidemic among young people, I should give a brief overview of the nature and history of adolescence as a background. It seems that 200 years ago, puberty and adolescence may have been inseparable events. Puberty, as a biological event, is marked by a system of hormonally induced somatic changes that renders the child sexually mature. Over the past 100 years, we have been aware of a progressively earlier onset of puberty in girls, reflected by the age at menarche (3). During that time, the average age of menarche has decreased from about fifteen to sixteen years to between eleven and twelve years now. Apparently, under the primary influence of improved nutrition, this trend is not easily detected in boys though there is reason to believe that it is occurring. It is reassuring to parents to know that this trend is tapering off, so we do not have to worry about explaining puberty to five-year-olds in the next century!

Adolescence, on the other hand, is a social phenomenon involving the preparation of the young for adult roles. In preindustrial societies adolescence as we know it today probably did not exist. As children became pubescent at fifteen or sixteen, they prepared to marry and work as adults. With the Industrial Revolution and continuing to the contemporary societal revolution of advanced technology, the period of preparation for adulthood has necessarily been extended to meet the needs of more complex work roles.

Musgrove captures the historical dilemma of adolescence well: "The adolescent was invented at the same time as the steam engine. The principal architect of the latter was Watt in 1765, of the former Rousseau in 1792. Having invented the adolescent, society has been faced with two major problems: how and where to accommodate him in the social structure, and how to make his behavior accord with the specifications. For two centuries English society has been involved in the problem of defining and clarifying the concept of precocity" (4, p. 33). Adolescence, which became significant in the early part of the nineteenth century, has lengthened by ten or even fifteen years, 150 years later. While growth and development have been enhanced by improved health care and nutrition, with the earlier onset of puberty as one of its manifestations and height and body size as others, the sexual and social maturation of behavior is delayed. And so we have biologically prepared, but socially immature, creatures whose awkwardness and emotional vulnerability are well known to all of us.

Turning now to the issue of this essay, a survey of the literature on delinquency presents us with a plethora of causative or associative factors, ranging from genetic potential to the degree of political stability existing at a given moment in history. In what follows, I will offer a selective evaluation of this literature without attempting to be exhaustive. The purpose of the evaluation will be to reach a practical and humanitarian understanding of the dilemma regarding violence in youth which will result in proposing an effective intervention.

**The Givens—What We Already Know**

In this section, I will consider the prevailing body of knowledge about adolescent socialization and social violence. First, I should review statistics that index how serious the increase in rates of lethal violence has become. The major causes of death for adolescents generally showed a decline up to 1960. This decline leveled off between 1960 and 1968 and then began to rise rapidly. The increasing mortality is taken up almost completely by motor vehicle accidents, homicide, and suicide, in that order (5).

Comparing motor vehicle accidents and homicides as specific causes of death among adolescents and young adults, it is of interest to note that the rate of increase for accidents began to accelerate around 1968 and continued to the early 1970s. The accident rate began to decelerate in 1973, presumably a result of the nationwide reduction in highway speed limits. A parallel acceleration in the rate of increase in homicide has occurred until the present.

Analysis of the homicide figures by race and sex reveals an important difference. The annual difference in homicide rates between nonwhite and white males rose from 61.3/100,000 to 107.7/100,000 over a five-year period between 1968 and 1973 (5). This is the largest disparity for all causes of death reported between any two comparison groups. While this represents an important finding, it appears that the rate of increase is similar between groups. I will not deal any more specifically with statistics except to say that numbers suggest that the availability of handguns, alcohol, and other drugs affecting the central nervous system are suspected correlates of the accelerating rate of violence in this age group. I might add that this is a plausible nonstatistical inference to make from routine newspaper reading.

Now I would like to examine three broad groups of factors, each of which has been independently thought to be a cause of violent behavior or, by more cautiously minded persons, has been assumed to interact in some as-yet-to-be-determined way to result in violent behavior. First, let us examine biological factors. For the most part, all these factors have their ultimate effect on the central nervous system and secondarily on behavior. The list of such factors or disorders has changed over the past years with evolution in psychology and the brain sciences. In terms of contemporary interest, I might list some which are of leading concern. These are epilepsy, minimal brain syndrome, the sex chromosomal aberration known as XXY, mental retardation, and learning disability. As a group of factors, we could ask if they are increasing in incidence. If their increase parallels the acceleration in rates of violence, we might examine such an association for its contributory value.

There is some indication that rates of mental retardation are increasing in society. This is partially the result of the increase in the survival of children with various mental retardation syndromes, mongoloidism assuming the greatest numerical importance in this list (6). Social labeling is probably a main contributor to the increase in mental retardation, through a process of glorifying the predictive power of intelligence tests and creating an entity known as mild mental retardation (7, p. 36). The overlap between this entity, learning disability, and delinquency is well established clinically, if not epidemiologically, but as far as I know there is no reason to expect those defined as retarded to be at an increased risk of lethal violence, in particular.

We have a pressing concern to find out if some forms of epilepsy (8), sex chromosomal variations (9), and minimal brain damage (10) are linked specifically to violence, but, thus far, in the search results have shown only "weak" associations at best. A major ethical and scientific problem is that these factors, depending on their severity, are relatively hidden from observation. Minimal brain damage may indeed be so minimal at times as to escape detection. The relative mental retardation ascribed to blacks on a genetic basis may not only be a cultural bias of intelligence tests, but, if I understand the recent suspicions developed around so much of the data collected by Cyril Burt and statistically elaborated by Jensen, the whole argument may be the result of one of the most amazing scientific heresies of this century (11).

To carry this argument further, the idea that violent people are categorically subject to a seizure disorder is difficult to rationalize if the seizures are subcortical and cannot be convincingly documented (or require esoteric and ethically questionable methods to attempt to document). I am admittedly being provocative by stating it in this way, but I wish to give you my interpretation of the literature on the episodic dyscontrol syndrome (and its variants) because of its popularity. The authors of *Violence and the Brain*, one of the leading treatises on the dyscontrol syndrome, did not restrain themselves from a provocative conclusion: ". . . It would be particularly interesting . . . to examine in detail those individuals who did cause serious injury or death in the Watts riot of 1965. It is important to keep in mind that each individual taking part in a riot has a unique life experience stored in his brain" (12, p. 151). This statement is meant to prevail upon the reader the potential contribution that psychosurgery may make to the problem of social violence. One reviewer of these various "hidden" biological indicators was so amazed by the strength of the argument and the weakness of the evidence that he coined this entire fascination the "new phrenology" (13). The importance of such hidden indicators is that they may be applied as labels without proof of their existence of linkage with violence. The public can be led to believe that such conditions are the cause of increased violence and readily accept as a justifiable response an extraordinary program of intervention.

I trust that you will not find this too much of a digression from the theme of adolescent socialization. Our concepts of violence inform our opinions as well as our treatments. It is conceivable to me that within ten or fifteen years chemical, surgical, and behavioral conditioning techniques will be the mainstays of our therapeutic armamentarium for violent offenders and that adolescents will represent a majority of persons so treated.

So as not to summarily dismiss such factors, I must contrast the evidence on the dyscontrol syndrome with that now accumulating on reading disability. It is not at all established that learning disability is a result of brain damage, but this is entirely possible. The overlap between reading disability and delinquency is quite large. At least, one investigator has thought that primary learning disability might be causally related to delinquency, through a sequence of events that begins with school failure and dropping out (14).

Despite a relative degree of plausibility that these biological factors are related to delinquency, and possibly violence, I suggest that they explain little in regard to our concern. Further, their intellectual fascination serves to drain resources that might be better applied elsewhere. This is especially true in the research field. Such factors also effectively divert public attention by stimulating scientific explanations that reinforce stereotypes regarding the inequality of our species. And, finally, these scientific formulations are perceived by the targeted group as vindictive and evil in intent.

The next broad category to examine is family deprivation. Can we explain increased rates of violent behavior as a result of increasing amounts of family pathology? Research studies and clinical work since the beginning of this century, subsumed under the name mental hygiene or child guidance movement, have continually found associations between delinquency and pathological family experiences, particularly experiences early in child development (15-17). From an ecological perspective, this seems as relevant now as it did at the onset of the industrial revolution. The stresses on family life are well established. The rising rate of divorce, separation, and desertion may well be a reflection of increased stress on family life. I am tempted to think that the rising rates of divorce and youthful violence are similar responses to factors which are gradually depreciating the quality of American family life.

If one looks at the kinds of intrafamilial experiences that have been found to correlate with delinquency, such as marital discord, father absence, repeated parental separations, lack of attachment, inconsistent discipline, and neglect and abuse of children, one must respect the powerful impact that such factors have on socialization of children. Yet, perhaps the major hypothesis emerging from this body of literature, that the roots of crime begin in early psychological deprivation, is without vigorous scientific justification (18). This may be partially a result of the many factors that must cluster together to constitute a "cause" or the many variations in outcome. One of the ways we are meeting the methodological challenge is in our statistical power of data analysis. Another, with which I am particularly fascinated, is how microscopic our attempts to define psychological deprivation have become. Take, for example, the work of Klaus and Kennell, which demonstrates how important physical contact between the mother and child is in the immediate hours after birth to their subsequent attachment (19). I am willing to admit that it may be weakness in the methods of social sciences and not their data alone which underlies the failure to demonstrate a causal relationship between family pathology and crime. This is a cautious opinion since I realize that there are a few very good studies and that as a clinician I seldom find a violent youth who has not been emotionally, if not physically, deprived in earlier life.

Before proceeding to the third group of factors, which are extrafamilial and sociological by definition, I wish to return to my previous discussion on the nature of adolescence as it relates to clinical practice. A concern I have had for some time about the family-deprivation hypothesis is the degree of closure it encourages. Let me illustrate. When a clinician is faced with evaluating a violent adolescent, his first ploy is to begin history taking. This may be an extensive exercise to reconstruct the child's past, his birth and development, failures, diseases, and traumas. Leaving the validity of such enterprises aside, this can be a telling retrospective prophecy. For when we find deprivation, we have an explanation. We proceed to formulate a plan to treat the deprivation. There are few satisfactory studies to judge the efficacy of psychological treatment, but it is my opinion that even in the best of circumstances the rehabilitation of adolescent offenders carries a high probability of failure when conventional psychotherapy is the major form of intervention.

What I wish to demonstrate here is how finding a sufficient historical explanation prevents further inquiry into the intellectual and emotional uniqueness of the adolescent person. (Of course, the same misgivings apply to the biological factors discussed above.) Understanding the significance of formal thought to early adolescence should assist us in realizing how the adolescent uses his emerging cognitive skills to evaluate his environment. The person is now equipped to become an active participant in the world of ideas, social contracts, and public policy. Adolescents are building long-range plans and projecting future images of themselves as adults (20). If this process goes unrecognized because of our nearsightedness to the adolescent person, we miss the opportunity to assist and support this phase of human development. Furthermore, when this inherent capacity is not appreciated or supported, the adolescent goes unchallenged, and bordom results.

Add to this concept of cognitive development at adolescence the lengthening period of socialization with its complex social and technical demands. This period is a limbo stretched between the expectable dependency of childhood and the responsibility of adulthood. It is an agonizing time for most people who enjoy the support of good families and schools. For those not so privileged, the adolescent's confrontation with the demands of adapting to a highly competitive, complex, racist environment is awesome.

The critical group of factors to explain increasing levels of lethal violence seem to be in the political, economic, and social order of our times. The adolescents' socialization toward violence is a final result of their intellectual examination of the environment and its possibilities for them. Many conclude, sometimes precipitously and sometimes after considerable inspection, that given the motivational demands, the number of years over which the demands are spread, and the competitiveness and complexity which must be dealt with constructively along the way that there are no reasonable objectives or rewards in society for them. They then resort to defeatist, given-up attitudes and compensatory face-saving tactics. I emphatically submit to you that it is this rational process that causes increasing numbers of adolescents to choose violent alternatives.

I can illustrate the process of adolsecent cognition by delineating a few questions which I think all adolescents, or preadolescents, between the ages of thirteen and sixteen years (excluding the severely retarded and brain damaged, of course) pose for themselves and their peer groups. They ask, What kind of society is this? What values control the activities of people? Where do I fit into the scheme of things? Do they (parents, teachers, police, and other adults) expect me to succeed or to fail? How much effort is demanded of me to do what they want me to do? Do I have the energy needed to meet the demand?

Imagine a child you know rather well—what answers would he give to these queries? The questions continue: Is there a way for me to get help (that is, develop the energy or obtain the resources) I need to meet the demand of socialization? What will happen if I don't make the effort? Exactly, what am I up against? If the adolescent meets with failure on these kinds of questions, he tries once more, desperately: Is there an action that will free me to think and act more clearly, more confidently in this society?

Whether or not the adolescent who reaches the conclusion that he will fail to meet the demands of socialization has a biological defect or a background of disturbed familial experiences seems meaningless when one can reach the conclusion based on real experiences that the channels of success are not worth the effort. Such factors are, at best, necessary but not sufficient conditions to explain violent behavior. But then again, I am not sure that they are even necessary conditions. Many minimally brain-damaged or emotionally deprived persons grow up to be productive members of our society. For instance, I am always surprised to find how many physicians claim to be dyslexic. Perhaps the experiences of early adolescence, and the way these experiences are understood by the person, are of such overriding importance that they overpower other presumed causal factors.

## The Not Givens—What We Do Not Know

I believe that our present concern with accelerating rates of lethal violence in young people is having an important impact on the sciences of sociology and psychology. We have been forced to admit our ignorance of adolescence as a unique period in human development, a period that is undergoing profound contemporary change. In this section I will discuss some of the important new directions that research in adolescent development is taking.

My discussion of the "new phrenology" (13) in the previous section attempted to persuade the reader that many biological factors which have been employed to explain delinquent behavior are minimally important, and possibly counterproductive, in our efforts to know the "truth."

To begin this discussion, I wish to raise the issue of biological factors again, but this time to suggest that they play a crucial role in adolescent socialization. By and large, we have taken the onset of puberty for granted. It is simply that age when girls begin to menstruate, boys begin to have "wet dreams," and both develop dimorphous secondary sex characteristics. In fact, there is quite a bit of variation in the timing of these hormonal and physiological events among children (21). This variation is likely to take on increased meaning as the interval between puberty as a biological phenomenon and adolescence as a social event is increased. The difference is likely to appear between early and late maturing children. One might expect that children who become pubescent between the ages of nine and eleven (the early maturing group) will be subject to greater psychological conflict than later maturing children (22).

The beginning of adolescence is less discrete than puberty. It is indicated by a role change—the child beginning to take responsibility for managing his life independently, though it is still recognized by his parents and society that he needs practice and support before finally becoming an adult (20). For some children this may occur at thirteen or fourteen years with starting a job, dropping out of school as an act of defiance, or becoming a parent. Other children may not really begin assuming even minimal responsibility for themselves until they leave home at seventeen or eighteen for college. The average age for beginning adolescence is probably around fifteen. Early maturing children may, therefore, have several years of being sexually prepared, in a biological sense, before assuming a role change that signifies the end of childhood.

In addition to the emotional conflict engendered, there may be other consequences of early versus late maturation. For example, a colleague of mine is currently examining cognitive differences between these groups. Her findings thus far suggest that late maturing children are superior on some aspects of cognitive functioning that may reflect a fairly subtle reorganization of the nervous system (23). This is a fruitful area of inquiry, one that allows for the integration of biological and social phenomena in a single explanatory paradigm.

Parallel with changes in cognition are changes in the use and meaning of language to adolescents. We know very little about this phenomenon, although we have been exposed for generations to the special vocabulary generated by adolescents. These new words have a way of becoming rapidly absorbed into common usage, and their regular appearance is a sure sign that adolescents are among us and that our linguistic world is steadily evolving. Delinquent adolescents, in particular, are commonly thought to be less verbal than their socialized peers. One of the postulates explaining delinquency is the need to rely on action because of a relative deficiency of language. I would suggest that the language deficiency thought to characterize the delinquent is a product of two phenomena. The first is the use of a culturally determined jargon which is undergoing a more idiosyncratic evolution than standard English (24). A second reason for the pseudodeficiency of delinquents' poor language skills is their need to convey more intense affect, usually anger, than their well-socialized peers. Indeed, the delinquent, particularly the violent delinquent, is challenged by the capacity of his language to act as a vehicle for his emotional reservoir.

We should assume that the complexity and meaningfulness of the delinquent's language is present though perhaps concealed. In what I consider one of the finest discussions I have read on psychotherapy with juvenile offenders, King (25) describes his experience in getting beyond the hostile, nonnegotiable remarks of adolescents to their profound feelings of anger and sadness. Once this is achieved, these children become not only more trusting as patients, but more articulate in expressing their ideas and concerns, as if some intellectual threshold were overcome.

Next, I should mention the important recent work of Nesselroade and Baltes (26) which has produced an important new addition to our understanding of adolescence, that is, the effect of historical change. The work is based on the assumption that adolescents are aware of their contemporary world, aware that history is in the making. They examined the possibility that the historical time of becoming an adolescent might be more important than chronological age as a determinant of personality. By studying children between the ages of eleven and seventeen between 1970 and 1972, they observed that children in 1970 (nearer the social upheaval of the late 1960s) were less ambitious and goal directed than children of similar age in 1972. The fact that they were able to get clear differences over such a short time interval, although a period of rapid social change, should be a stimulus to study longer time intervals for their specific effects on the integration of personality in adolescents. Their work also serves to underscore what my main theme is in this paper, that arriving at a formal cognitive understanding of society is a crucial task of adolescent socialization.

Up to this point, I have discussed broad factors that are relevant to a general appreciation of adolescence. For the remainder of this section, I wish to point out the research needs that may help us in reducing the rate of violent behavior among youth.

First, we need to improve our understanding of the precursors or predictors of violence in preadolescent children. Much of what I have already said about specific developmental changes attendant on beginning adolescence suggests that this problem of preadolescent prediction is no easy matter. Traditionally, the triad of behavior, fire setting, enuresis, and cruelty to animals, is thought to be adequate predictive criteria. While finding all three in one child might be safe, on clinical grounds, to predict violence, one has to look hard and long to find enough children with the triad to study the predictive validity. The search for a satisfactory behavioral profile of the preadolescent who later becomes a delinquent is an unfinished business in psychiatry. From time to time new proposals are offered, but to date the kind of prospective, longitudinal studies ultimately needed to answer such questions have not been done.

A well-designed study by a British research group partially meets this need. The study indicates that family factors such as unemployment and marital discord may account for a greater percentage of the variance in predicting who becomes delinquent than the predelinquent behavior of the children (27). Certainly, the longer the interval over which an attempt is made to predict delinquency or violence, the more risky and less successful the process is likely to be. I am not attempting to be contradictory by first claiming that family deprivation may be only a minor determinant in the socialization toward violence and then encouraging more research in the area. What I am stating is that researchers who undertake such enterprises should be as prepared to find that lack of success in long-range prediction as they are to find continuities from predelinquency to delinquency (or previolence to violence).

This brings us to situational factors that may determine the context of violence. Drugs, especially those that depress central nervous system functioning, are known to induce regression in behavior generally. Of course, psychoanalytic theory would inform us that putting any pill, cigarette, or mood-changing drink into the mouth is regressive. I do not know of conclusive data which links drug use to violence. Opiates can be considered linked to crime by the profit motive. Central nervous system stimulant drugs, like the amphetamines and cocaine, may have a more specific endogenous effect on the induction of aggressive behavior in the user (28). The threshold for such an effect may be heightened by an intermittent or random use of the drug which is more characteristic of adolescents than adults. We need much more information on drug effects and patterns of usage before we can comfortably build an association with violence.

Other situational factors, belabored by the press, are the availability of handguns, the production of dangerous automobiles, and the prevalence of pornography. All these have become routine, expectable parts of our daily lives as presented to us by the media. Aside from acting as situational stimuli to violence, one must be concerned about their social learning value in young children. It seems beyond debate that we are a society that encourages aggression. While the primary value of this kind of stimulation and education may be to ensure that we remain consumers in the market place, secondary effect may, in fact, be an unwanted increase in crime and violence.

Another area for improved understanding is in the area of rehabilitation and prognosis of youthful violence. We need more information on when immature expressions of violence characteristic of adolescence lead to continued immature behavior in the adult on the one hand, and when it leads to mature expressions of violence, such as organized crime, police brutality, and warfare, on the other. The former description fits the psychiatric diagnosis of an anti-social character disorder. The other, much more subtle and insidious in its long-term effects on society, may be just as important to the mastery of our social constructions over disorganization, anomie, and chaotic living conditions as the first.

Let me share with you briefly an overview of our experience in Boston. As a consultant to the Boston Region of the Department of Youth Services (the juvenile correctional agency) for the Commonwealth of Massachusetts, I recently made an informal survey of how many children are now in custody for acts of lethal violence, and what attitudes and opinions are possessed by the social workers who manage their lives. Of approximately forty-three children in custody for homicide, attempted murder, rape, suicide, lethal confrontation with a law officer, and car theft (resulting in a lethal accident), the child rapists are considered to have the poorest prognosis and are thought to be the most treatment resistant. Recidivism is high in this group, and the workers are often confused by the socially conforming and quiet, passive behavior of these children.

All the workers are aware that the rate of lethal violence has increased, easily three times since 1970 (this is consistent with the national trend). If we add to this category those children charged with armed robbery or aggravated assault, we increase the number of children now in custody to well over 100, constituting about 40 percent of all children in custody. It is recognized that the psychological makeup of these children has not changed as much as our social norms have. In discussing the objectives of this essay with them, they expressed to me the belief that two important factors are related to the increase in lethal violence in Boston. First, there is the general phenomenon of fragmenting social control and a loss of rational authority. Second, they observe that many adolescents have arrived at a socially shared belief that the "price of life" is cheap.

For this group the concern for increasing rates of violence is matched by a concern for increasingly sensational acts of violence. The majority of children in custody are black, but as a group they are not qualitatively more violent than white children. In our staff training conferences, we reflect on how many of these children are learning disabled or sexually immature (despite the fact that many are fathers and mothers), how boring their daily lives are, and how most cannot find jobs or training experiences even if they try. Finally, we fret over how impotent we are to change their lives, how often we disagree with the courts, and how fragmented and self-serving our human services system is.

The final, and in many ways most important, research need we have is the epidemiology and human ecology of violence. Examination of the prevalence and incidence of violent behavior should be related to the study of urban demography. Such familiar demographic variables as age structure, family size, rate of unemployment, and housing conditions should be expanded to include the occurrence of stressful life events (29), access to human service needs, and social support systems (30).

The seminal work of Shaw and McKay (31) in the 1930s provides important groundwork for such an inquiry. Their work demonstrated a predictable relationship between rates of delinquency and urban topography in several American cities. With a changing urban landscape, and new relationships between urban and suburban areas, a replication of this work may reveal some new and interesting findings. Also, the physical sense of topography (housing, open spaces, traffic patterns, concentration of pollutants) needs to be expanded to include the forms and content of information in the environment. If my general thesis is correct, that adolescents are entering a new developmental phase of intellectual awareness, and that this new learning is important to the organization and control of their behavior, then the addition of this dimension to urban topography is critically important to the development of a more sophisticated comprehension of adolescent socialization.

Before completing this section, I should mention the work of one of the few American epidemiologists concentrating his effort in the field of child psychiatry. The research group at Columbia directed by Thomas Langner is currently publishing work of a cross-sectional longitudinal study of children from New York City (32-34). An important contribution of their work represents the contrast of children from the general population with children of parents on welfare. Their results indicate many more similarities than would have been expected between these groups on dimensions of child behavior and parent-child interaction. An important finding that distinguishes the groups is the presence of greater numbers of delinquent children in the welfare sample. This appeared to be specifically related to paternal coldness in their parent-child relationships (33). In combination with other studies (35), this suggests we should reexamine the theme of maternal deprivation in our theories of character development and devote greater attention to the possible contributions of paternal deprivation.

## Final Thoughts and Recommendations for Action

I have argued that the socialization of adolescents is essentially an experience in reconstructing the social order through a process of newly acquired cognitive facility, what Piaget has called the period of "formal thought." Obviously, children differ in the degree of conformity and creativity with which they approach adolescence. The end results of the adolescent's reconstruction is either to join the social order or, through a process of social depreciation and boredom, to slide into a life course characterized by an absence of planning and social disorder (36).

Given all the information needed to understand youthful violence, we might be faced with the fact that many, perhaps the majority of, adolescents have the urge to act violently. This tendency toward violent behavior is no more than the routine frustration we all experience from time to time as a result of living in a highly competitive, frequently threatening society that sensationalizes violence. Once an adolescent develops and understands the proposition that in order to survive and succeed in this environment one must be aggressive, the actual occurrence of his lethal violence may be more the result of the context in which he acts than his "premorbid" background.

Epidemiologists and ecologists should eventually be able to tell us more about how different environments represent different contexts in which behavior is manifested. Such socially protective strategies as making it difficult to purchase handguns or drugs and the control or elimination of cigarettes and alcohol advertisements may produce contexts in which rates of violence are relatively low. As well, the characterization of neighborhoods as integrated or disintegrated, using something like the propositions of Leighton (37), may be an adequate construct to account for differences in rates and levels of violence. I am most impressed with recent attempts to develop a theory of neighborhood support systems. The frequency of casual and organized contact between neighborhood members, or household-kin-friend networks as Epling, Vandale, and Stewart (38) term them, is likely to have important educational and cooperative influences in a community.

The major part of the burden for action should fall upon the schools. They carry the responsibility and technical skill to support and stimulate adolescent intellectual development. Assisting the adolescent in formulating and negotiating in an active way his propositions about the world is a function few schools attain. For most youngsters there is an urgent need for sex education, drug education, demography, national politics, and foreign affairs. Most, if not all, of these lessons we believe them to be too young to learn. How to make a loan, choose a car, contact your political representatives, and so on are tasks they need to validate their appreciation of the real world of economics, health, politics, and propaganda. Without adequate tests of their propositions they become educationally deprived. Rather than postulate school refusal as a factor of poor adjustment, perhaps we ought to view it as an adolescent means of reasoning through real experiences to a conclusion which is not illogical despite its social undesirability. I have often envisioned a course on the history of adolescence given as a requirement of high school graduation. Young people need some formal appreciation of how their own social and emotional changes, as complex as they are in contemporary society, fit a historical perspective.

Decrease the rate of school dropout by transforming education to the real world needs and developmental stage of adolescents and there will be a proportional decrease in crime and delinquency. I appreciate that this is a mundane recommendation, but as long as it lies within our means to control the educational process and we fail as a society to make needed changes in our schools, then it deserves repetition. While I assure you that I have a healthy respect for biological differences and for psychopathology, I do not believe that solving our social problems will result from the control of such factors. Adolescent violence is but an immature expression of adult violence. As a society prepared for violence, we will stimulate our children to think and know about it and heighten the chances that some will act violently. A society that depreciates the dignity of some members of the species, as we do through racism, classism, nationalism, and religious orders, will create undignified persons. We are right to be critically concerned about the violent and undignified because they challenge, in their knowing and acting, our constant worry about deterioration in the social order.

I have consciously avoided emphasis on racial differences. I believe that adolescence has become a universal experience and that our environment stimulates any human being developing in it to create similar kinds of ideas and actions. We are discussing differences of quantity more than quality in our concern for rates and levels of violence. If we are forced to focus our attention on racial differences, then all we can do is acknowledge that it will take a greater and more sustained effort to lower the level of lethal violence in blacks than whites. But the methods and tools must be qualitatively the same, and they must be concentrated in our schools.

The importance of the media, advertising, and educational deprivation is merely to give adolescents "food for thought." The control of violence is dependent upon a reexamination by all of us on what purpose is served by stimulating aggression or, as an ecological problem, by differentially stimulating aggression in society.

Science and public policy have important, though perhaps different, roles to play in assisting us to solve this problem. Our responsibility in either case is to construct a viable and enduring social order, one that will reestablish the integrity of adolescence as a critical phase in the life cycle (39). I believe that in our effort to control violence we are in a historical predicament not unlike our predecessors in this country whose challenge it was to control hunger and infectious disease. It is my belief that our capacity to meet this challenge is intact. The contribution of medicine, psychiatry, and the biological sciences is an important one, but we must insist on a noncompromising humanism to complement our scientific vigor.

## References

1. P.L. Berger and T. Luckman. The social construction of reality. New York: Doubleday, 1967.

2. G. Breitman, ed. Malcolm X speaks. New York: Grove, 1966.

3. J.M. Tanner. Growth at adolescence. London: Blackwell, 1962.

4. F. Musgrove. Youth and the social order. London: Routledge & Kegan Paul, 1964.

5. N.S. Weiss. Am. J. Epidemiol. 103(4):416, 1976.

6. N. Goodman and J. Tizard. Br. Med. J. 1:216, 1962.

7. J. Mercer. Labeling the mentally retarded. Berkeley: Univ. California Press, 1973.

8. I. Philips and N. Williams. Am. J. Psychiatry 132:1265, 1975.

9. M.D. Carey. Lancet 2:859, 1966.

10. M. Menkes, J. Rowen, and J. Menkes. Pediatrics 39:393, 1967.

11. Times (London), October 21, 1976.

12. V. Mark and F. Ervin. Violence and the brain. New York: Harper & Row, 1970.

13. L.S. Coleman. Am. J. Orthopsychiatry 44(5):675, 1974.

14. M. Rutter and W. Yule. J. Child Psychol. Psychiatry 16:181, 1975.

15. C. Burt. The young delinquent. London: Univ. London Press, 1925.

16. W. Healy and A.F. Bronner. New light on delinquency and its treatment. New Haven, Conn.: Yale Univ. Press, 1936.

17. S. Glueck and E. Glueck. Unraveling juvenile delinquency. New York: Commonwealth Fund, 1950.

18. W. McCord and J. McCord. The origins of crime. New York: Columbia Univ. Press, 1959.

19. M. Klaus and J. Kennell. Maternal-infant bonding. St. Louis: Mosby, 1976.

20. B. Inhelder and J. Piaget. The growth of logical thinking: from childhood to adolescence. New York: Basic, 1958.

21. R. Frisch. In: M.M. Grumbach, G.D. Crane, and F.E. Mayer, eds. Control and onset of puberty. New York: Wiley, 1974.

22. L. Kohlberg and C. Gilligan, Daedulus 100(4):1051, 1971.

23. D. Waber. Dev. Psychol. 13:29, 1977.

24. J. Dillard. Black English. New York: Random, 1972.

25. C. King. Am. J. Orthopsychiatry 45(1):134, 1975.

26. J. Nesselroade and P. Baltes. Adolescent personality development and historical change: 1970-1972. Monogr. Soc. Res. Child Dev., no. 154, 39(1), 1974.

27. D.J. West. Who becomes delinquent? London: Heineman, 1973.

28. R. Post and R. Kopanda. Am. J. Psychiatry 133:627, 1976.

29. J. Rabkin and E. Struening. Science 194:1013, 1976.

30. J. Cassel. Int. J. Health Serv. 4(3):537, 1974.

31. C. Shaw and H. McKay. Juvenile delinquency and urban areas. Chicago: Univ. Chicago Press, 1942.

32. J. Eisenberg, J. Gersten, T. Langner, et al. Am. J. Orthopsychiatry 46: 447, 1976.

33. J. Eisenberg, T. Langner, J. Gersten. Arch. Behav. Sciences 48:1, 1975.

34. T. Langner, J. Gersten, E. Greene, et al. J. Consult. Clin. Psychol. 42: 170, 1974.

35. F. Earls. Psychiatry 39:209, 1976.

36. L. Eisenberg and F. Earls. In: D. Hamburg and K. Brodie, eds. American handbook of psychiatry, vol. 6. New York: Basic, 1975.

37. A.L. Leighton. My name is legion. New York: Basic, 1959.

38. P. Epling, S. Vandale, and G. Stewart. In: S. Engman and A Thomas, eds. Topias and utopias in health. Chicago: Aldine, 1975.

39. B. Hamburg. In: G.V. Coelho, D.A. Hamburg, and J.E. Adams, eds. Coping and adaptation. New York: Basic, 1975.

# 5
# Cultural Sanctions of Urban Homicide

*Henry P. Lundsgaarde*

This essay touches on three critical aspects of urban violence in contemporary America: the increase in crimes of violence against persons, the decrease in apprehension and punishment of the perpetrators of such violence, and the general belief that the system of criminal justice effectively balances individual rights with the society's need for justice. With regards to the last, the findings from my study of homicide in Houston imply that any scientific explanation of urban violence must consider the total cultural context in which violence occurs.

A few words first about the four homicide cases that follow. Three of these cases, which have been extracted from the official records of the Houston Police Department, have been previously described in *Murder in Space City*. The fourth case, which involves a contract murder, has been exhaustively described in Thompson's *Blood and Money*. The names of all the principals, except for those described by Thompson, have been changed.

Each case from 1969 typifies a different killer-victim relationship. An awareness of these relationships and of the context in which the killing occurs is necessary but not sufficient for understanding the judicial outcome in all cases. One must also know the cultural sanctions that determine the judicial outcomes for killers.

The recent 1974 Texas Penal Code, with few exceptions, formally omits both the killer-victim relationship and the situation from the statutes intended to insure a match between the type of offense and its punishment. However, informally, the killer's legal penalty, if any, is closely related to a subjective judicial assessment of his "state of mind" and his purported motive. The data show that in cases where an offender's "state of mind" is "passionate" and when the context of killing implies self-defense, that officials devote only cursory attention to homicide. If, on the other hand, it is possible to relate the killing to achievement of another goal, such as rape or theft, the authorities may maximize their efforts to punish the culprit. The available data also reveal that Texas lawmakers have so far felt it unnecessary to significantly change parts of the Penal Code pertaining to the broad privilege of individuals to use violence in defense of person or property because the existing statutory laws accurately

I wish to express my thanks to Johanna Shaw, M.D., and the organizer and participants in the conference on Legal Aspects of Urban Violence.

mirror the social values, beliefs, and general attitudes of the public sanctioning
such violence.


## The Common-Law Wife

[Carolyn] A white woman age 25, and a Mexican-American woman, age
22, were both charged with the death of the elder woman's common-law
husband [Mike], age 42. [Mike] was the owner of a striptease club in
which his wife worked as a stripper. [Mike and Carolyn] had a reputation for fighting. On August 2, 1969, the husband hired a new striptease
performer—the 22-year-old woman. The new stripper had no place to
stay and she was therefore invited by the club owner to stay with him
and his common-law wife. Sometime after this arrangement was established the husband disappeared. Neighbors reported to the police that
they had seen the two women remove a large steamer trunk on August
5th from the apartment and had become suspicious because the man had
not parked in his assigned parking lot or told anyone he was going on
vacation. Both women were apprehended by the police on August 6th
and the younger woman submitted a written affidavit. The following
excerpts from this affidavit express some remarkable views of life and
human relationships:

I went to work on Saturday, August 2, 1969, and after work I went to
Carolyn's and Mike's apartment. . . . I thought the door was locked but
all of a sudden it opened and Mike came into the apartment. I kind of
gave him a dirty look and I told him I was not going to do it [relay a
message from Mike to Carolyn]. He had sent Carolyn out to get some
7-Up before he told me this. . . . After [finishing my bath] I came out
and a little later Carolyn and her small boy, who had a branch in his
hand, came into the apartment. The little boy had been crying. I [saw]
a bruise on the boy's face and asked what it was and she said it was just
a bruise. In a little while I left and went across the street to the drug-
store in the shopping center. I left the shopping center and I started
back toward the apartment. When I passed by the club I felt hungry
and I went into the Mexican restaurant which is next door to the club.
I had been in the restaurant for a little while and while I was eating Mike
came in and sat down next to me. He just sat there and did not say anything until I told him, "You sure are quiet." He said, "I sure am." We
didn't say much more and I finished eating and paid my bill and went
back to the apartment. I went to work Monday. When I got off work
Carolyn and I were supposed to take a new girl home. We had to go by
the apartment to get my glasses and we found the door locked and could
not get in. We tried the window and Mike came out and asked what was
going on. I told him that I had to get my glasses and that we were going
to take this girl home. . . . He did not say anything else and I went in
and got my glasses. It was close to 1 A.M. and we did not get back until
about 3 A.M. and Mike had [again] locked the door and windows so
that we could not get into the apartment. We went over to the club and
stayed there during the night. We got up at 8 or 9 A.M. and went over
to the apartment. Carolyn had to remove a glass pane to get into the

apartment. After we got inside I went to the bedroom and shut the door.
I then overheard an argument and a little later I heard the first shot.
After the first shot I went into the living room. I then heard another
shot. Carolyn came running out of the bedroom and said, "Let's get out
of here!" I ran with her and we went over to stay with her son's baby-
sitter. On the way over she said that she had shot Mike and if I thought
that he might be dead [they returned to the apartment and Carolyn
threw her .38 caliber pistol away]. . . . When we got back to the apartment and into the bedroom, I looked at Mike and he appeared to be dead.
Carolyn then felt him and said, "He is dead." We sat around for a while
and it was then time for the club to open and we took the money over
to the club and opened the club. We sat around for a while and I was so
shook up so Carolyn said, "Let's go shopping!" We then went back to
the apartment and checked on him again and he was still lying where we
had left him. We then locked the apartment and were trying to decide
how to get Mike's body out of the apartment. Carolyn just wanted to
take him like he was and to drop him but I thought that a trunk would
be better. We then went to some store and bought a large trunk. . . .
We then went back to the apartment and brought the trunk inside. We
sat down and fixed ourselves a drink and were trying to think how we
could get him into the trunk. We placed the trunk beside him and
Carolyn pushed him into the trunk. . . . Before we closed the trunk,
Carolyn noticed Mike's face and she screamed and said, "Put something
over his face." I got a towel and put it over his face. She closed the lid.
We went back to work at the club and stayed there until closing time
after midnight. We then went back to the apartment to discuss about
the best time to take him out and dump him. Carolyn said about 3 A.M.
We went outside the apartment several times and acted as if we were
looking for Mike because we knew that people would begin to ask questions and to start looking for Mike. We tried to clean up the blood. We
first tried to place the trunk on Carolyn's son's toy wagon but it wouldn't
hold. . . . We parked the car close to the apartment and dragged the
trunk across to the car where we placed it on the back seat. We drove
off to try to find a place to dump the body. . . . We . . . drove down a
road until it came to a dead end [they returned briefly to a store where
Carolyn left the car to buy some lighter fluid] . . . and we drove through
a gate into the woods where we got out. It took us a long time to get
the trunk out of the car. Carolyn tilted the trunk so that Mike's body
fell out on the ground and I put a sheet over the body. We then pulled
the trunk back away from the car and also placed our purses back away
from the car. Carolyn then poured the lighter fluid over the sheet on
the body. She lighted a match, started a fire and we grabbed the empty
trunk and ran. . . . The only reason I helped Carolyn was because she
said she would give me $1,000 to help her.

Carolyn later led the police to the place were the body had been
dumped. Autopsy revealed that Mike had died of a gunshot wound in
the chest. Carolyn was arrested and indicted for murder. She was tried
and found to be *not guilty* on June 22, 1970. Her assistant was charged
and indicted for the same offense but there is no information about the
outcome in her case. (Lundsgaarde 1977: 81-84)

**The Cuckold**

The killer, Mr. Jones, a 27-year-old White male, and his wife, age 32, had been very good friends of the victim, Mr. Russell, age 47, until the fatal episode that took place around midnight some time in October, 1969. When the police arrived at the scene of the killing they were met by Mr. Jones who calmly informed them that "I caught him with my wife and I shot him." The weapon, a .22 caliber rifle, was on top of the car in which Mr. Russell was shot. The relationships . . . [among] the three principals, together with the final events leading to the homicidal episode, are vividly summarized in an affidavit submitted to the police by the principal eyewitness, Mrs. Jones:

Last night, at about 11:30 P.M., I called Russell at his home. I called to ask if I could borrow some money from him to pay the rent and the utilities. He said that he would lend me the money and [that] he would let me have about $55. He said he would be over as soon as he found a service station open as his tank was nearly empty. I guess it was about five minutes to midnight when he got to my house. I opened the front door and told him to come in. He said, "No, it's late and I have to get on back home." After he said this he walked up on the porch and we were just standing there talking about different things and the troubles me and Jones were having. About this time Russell made some remark about my husband being down at some joint watching go-go girls and that he could not stay as he had to work in the morning. About this time some cars passed [the house] and Russell said that I was going to be the talk of the neighborhood because I was standing out front talking to a bachelor. I said, "Let's go in the living room," but Russell said he wouldn't and that it wouldn't look too good so he said, "Let's just sit in the car and talk for a few minutes." We got in the car and talked for a few minutes. After a little while Russell teased me about how my hair looked and he kissed me a few times and then I kissed him back a few times. I kidded him about wrinkling his white shirt and he said that he wasn't worried about his shirt and that it was his tight black pants that were bothering him. This is when he said he would get comfortable and that's when he pulled his pants down around his knees. His shorts were down, too. When he said his pants were too tight, I told him to let me see and I felt and he had an erection. This is when he pulled his pants down and he took his left leg out of his britches. He then reached over and kissed me. At this time I was sitting under the steering wheel and Russell was over on the passenger's side. This is when Russell told me, "It's too late to send me home now." He reached over and kissed me. About this time I looked over Russell's shoulder and saw my husband. He had a gun. I think it was a .22 caliber rifle and my husband said something and then Russell said, "Now listen, Jones" or "Wait, Jones" and this is when my husband shot him. I jumped out of the car and ran around the front and my husband had the gun pointed at me. I asked him not to shoot me and to think of our daughter. Then he said he wasn't going to kill me and that I wasn't fit to kill and that he was just going to beat the hell out of me. He then hit me in the face and grabbed me by the arm. I pulled away from him and looked into the car and saw Russell. He was bleeding real bad from the back of his head and he vomited. I hollered

for my husband to call an ambulance but he said, "It's no use, he is dead."
I ran into the house and called an ambulance but my husband jerked the
phone out of my hand and said that he would call and that he would
also call the cops. I grabbed a wet towel from the bathroom and went
back to the car and started to wipe stuff off of Russell's face and then I
put the rag behind his head. About this time the police arrived and I
went back into the house to quiet my children. I told my son to keep
the other children in the bedroom.

The follow-up police investigation revealed that Jones and Russell had
worked for the same tool manufacturing company for several years.
They worked different shifts, however. The adulterous relationship had
started about two years before the killing and the Joneses were good
friends with Russell as was made evident by their mutual get togethers
for picnics and fishing. The couple also owned a houseboat together
with Russell. According to Mrs Jones, she and Russell managed to see
each other privately and to have intercourse about three times a week.
She had expressed a desire for a divorce but the couple had not separated
or taken formal steps to dissolve the marriage.

Mr. Jones was charged with murder and brought before a grand jury. He
was not billed and released from police custody. A letter from the
assistant district attorney, addressed to the Homicide Division, informed
the police of the outcome of the case and it further instructed the police
to release the rifle to Mr. Jones. It must be added that Mr. Jones, who
certainly must have been motivated by passion, had suspected his wife
and his friend. On the eve of the killing he had told Russell that he was
going up to Lake Houston and Russell, in turn, had told him that he was
going home. The two men had been drinking beer together at a lounge.
Mr. Jones changed his mind about his trip and as he returned home he
spotted the car in his driveway. He drove his car past his house, parked it,
and took his rifle from the car and walked toward the house. He looked
into the parked car, saw the couple, and fired. The ready availability of
the means to kill, the rifle, was not noted anywhere in the police report.
But why should a loaded rifle in a personal car be raised as an issue,
when as is generally known, it is a common and socially acceptable form
of behavior to carry personal weapons?

Jones' early release from police custody certainly could not fail to signal
the righteousness of his act to his children, his wife, their neighbors, and
—as the story was disseminated by the news media—ultimately to the
city populace at large. Those who argue that "law" and "custom" are sep-
arable realities or domains must, it seems, base their argument on seman-
tic niceties rather than facts. (Lundsgaarde 1977: 107-109)

## The Unyielding Motorist

The facts of the following case were established on the basis of the killer's
affidavit together with those by his wife and mistress. In his own words:

On March 15th, I went to Bob's Cafe and picked up my wife. She works
at this cafe as a waitress and gets off work at 12:00 midnight. I had

picked up my wife and we started home. I was driving south on Brewster Street when a car ran a stop sign and hit the rear end of my car. . . . I then followed this car. When we reached Collingsworth Street the man stopped his car and we stopped directly behind him. After we had stopped the car I got my knife. It was lying on the floor of my car and I picked it up and put it in my pocket. I then got out of my car and went up to the other car. . . . The man was still sitting in his car behind the steering wheel. I asked the man, ". . . [Mister,] how come you hit my car and are taking off like that?" At this time the man started cussing at me and he got out of his car. He had his hand in his pocket and he continued to cuss me. After he got out of his car he still had his hand in his pocket and he backed up to the rear of his car. When he got to the rear end of the car he had his hand out of his pocket and there was an open knife in it. At this time I got my knife from my pocket. . . . The man started to swing his knife and he cut my left arm a little. . . . I then cut at this man and I think I cut him on the face. He staggered back and started to change hands with the knife. Then the man came at me again and knocked me down and knocked my knife out of my hand. Some way or another I managed to get the knife off the ground and then he came back at me and I had started getting up off the ground and I stabbed him. I don't know just how many times. After I stabbed him he staggered back to the side of his car and leaned over it. He was looking at me but he didn't say anything. . . . I told my wife, "Let's go!" and we left. My wife had gotten out of the car and I went and picked up Marilyn as she was at her aunt's house. I drove Marilyn to her house and I told her about the stabbing on the way to her house. . . . On my way home I drove down past the street where the incident had occurred and I looked to see if the car was still there. It was not. I thought that the man was all right and I went on home. . . .

The killer's wife corroborated the facts of the story. The girl friend's testimony, had it ever come to that, would of course have been viewed as hearsay and therefore inadmissible evidence in a criminal trial. The case never did go to trial because the grand jury declined to indict the killer on the basis of the facts summarized in the preceding paragraphs. The weapon, incidentally, was a fair-sized hunting knife. (Lundsgaarde 1977: 128–129)

## The Debutante, the Surgeon, and the Oil Baron

The exact cause of death in 1969 of Mrs. Joan Robinson Hill, former debutante and wife of Dr. John Hill, remains a mystery. No less than two separate autopsies of Mrs. Hill's remains were conducted to discover the cause of her sudden death and, more importantly, to reveal if her death could be attributed to foul play on the part of her surviving and estranged husband. Following the first autopsy procedure, which was conducted by one of Houston's foremost experts on forensic pathology, the deceased woman's father, Mr. Ash Robinson, managed to persuade the authorities that a second autopsy should be performed. This time the autopsy was performed by a forensic pathol-

ogist brought in from New York. This physician was paid directly for
his services by Mr. Robinson. The results of the second autopsy were as
inconclusive as the first one, however. Despite the failure of the two
autopsy investigations to yield any data which would implicate any
other person in Mrs. Robinson Hill's sudden death, a Houston grand
jury moved to indict Dr. John Hill for the murder of his wife. Dr. Hill
went to trial and was acquitted. The father-in-law, who openly professed
that he believed Dr. Hill to have killed his daughter, was unsatisfied by
the outcome of the trial. Dr. John Hill could not be tried twice for the
same offense and his father-in-law knew that other avenues of avenge had
to be pursued. Mr. Robinson set out to ruin Dr. Hill's reputation as a
skillful plastic surgeon in the community and he forced the son-in-law
into a series of complex legal battles over the ownership of property and
guardianship of his own grandson and Dr. Hill's son.

Matters were resolved when Dr. Hill was subsequently killed in the immediate presence of his mother, his son, and his third wife. The murder
occurred in Dr. Hill's home and the killer, who was never apprehended
by the police, made no effort to steal any valuables from the household.
The killing was characterized by the Houston police as a contract
murder. The suspected killer was sometime later located in a Dallas bar
where he quite accidentally was killed during a brawl with a police
officer. A weak link in the chain of evidence which could connect Mr.
Robinson with Dr. Hill's murderer was found in the person of a Mrs.
Lilla Paulus. Mrs. Paulus, who was acquainted with both Mr. Robinson
and Dr. Hill's alleged murderer, was arrested and tried as an accomplice
in the Hill murder case. She was found guilty by a jury and sentenced to
thirty-five years' imprisonment. The originator of the contract killing,
according to the evidence presented by Thompson, went completely un-
scathed. Rumor now has it that the author of *Blood and Money* may
have invited the issuing of a murder contract on his own life because of
his free use of personal names and serious allegations about the role of
Mr. Ash Robinson in the entire sordid story about the wheelings and
dealings of the principals connected to the John Hill murder case. The
Hill case is fascinating in and of itself because it contains all the ingredi-
ents of a good murder mystery. Although it is easy to quarrel with many
of Thompson's conclusions, particularly those founded on his inference
about the feelings and attitudes of the people most directly involved
with the Hill case, it is evident that the influence and the affluence of the
victims resulted in more official attention than is customarily accorded a
Houston homicide case. Although the Houston grand jury moved cautiously and slowly before it indicted Dr. John Hill for the murder of his
wife, other grand juries have been clocked to spend only minutes on
hearing and dismissing the evidence from cases involving more substantial information than was evident in the Hill case. The offenses committed by less affluent and attractive citizens in the community rarely
catch the careful attention that such cases might deserve. A casual and
unguarded comment by a member of a Houston grand jury provides an
important clue to the explanation of why homicide cases, like the four
cases described above, receive differential attention from both the public
and legal authorities. In his own words: "We kind of looked forward to
the rape and sodomy cases and stuff like that because they broke the

routine. I mean if you've heard one bad check case, you've heard them all. But the unusual cases were a little more interesting, and we kind of took our time with them." (Carp 1974: 119).


## Sanctions

The definition of culture as ". . . all those historically created designs for living . . . which exist at any given time as potential guides for the behavior of men" (Kluckholn and Kelly 1945: 97), provides an important point of departure for the discovery of how different sanctions function to regulate different social behavior.

Sanctions, which symbolize cultural approval or disapproval, can be conceptualized as servomechanisms that enable both individuals and institutions to regulate social behavior. The four cases presented here illustrate how individual members in one particular culture may, given certain social circumstances, employ lethal force to regulate the actions and behaviors of other people. The case of the cuckold perhaps most directly illustrates how one individual may enforce his concept of right or wrong social behavior upon others. What makes this case, and many others like it, interesting is that the sanctioning behavior of the individual and the more abstract institutional sanctions of the legal system are linked.

To understand both how and why so many individuals in this culture employ violence as a mode of conflict resolution *and* escape official punishment, we must look to the institutional supports and cultural guidelines that positively sanction the private use of force. The most immediately visible demonstration of the sanctioning process is to be found in the decision-making procedures of the grand jury.

The grand jury system has a long and fascinating intellectual history with deep roots in Anglo-Saxon and English law. The fundamental purpose of the modern-day grand jury is to receive complaints and accusations in criminal cases. The grand jury, which in Texas is made up of twelve members, hears evidence presented by the state and decides whether that evidence calls for a formal indictment. If the grand jury issues an indictment against a defendant the case will be tried in a court of law. If, on the other hand, the grand jury decides that the evidence presented to it does not warrant further official legal action, it will issue a "no bill" and thus remove a defendant from any further consideration by the legal authorities.

Grand jury members are not experts on law. Their lack of expertise is supposed to insure defendants against tyrannical actions by the state and its representatives in the judiciary. The grand jury, therefore, is a group of ordinary citizens who are asked to decide whether the actions of one of their fellow citizens should be sanctioned by governmental authorities.

A brief examination of the membership composition of the Harris County Grand Jury partly explains why fewer than one-half of all the cases brought to its attention result in an indictment. The members of the Harris County Grand Jury, according to Professor Carp, who served on one grand jury and made a study of its deliberations, are not representative of the general Houston populace. Carp notes that the members of the grand jury are white, college educated, professionals or business executives with annual personal incomes above $25,000. The Houston populace, on the other hand, is approximately 69 percent white, 11 percent Mexican-American, and 20 percent black. The median level of education for the city populace is twelve years of school and the median family income is $10,348. The grand jury members, therefore, are not as representative of the general citizenry as judicial idealists would hope.

According to Thompson's study of the Hill case(s) the grand jury should have issued a no bill in favor of Dr. John Hill. Thompson implies that the foreman persuaded the members of his grand jury that the plastic surgeon should be indicted despite the lack of evidence because of personal friendship between the jury foreman and Ash Robinson. This serves to illustrate how unusual circumstances may force a grand jury to behave in an unusual and unpredictable way.

Professor Carp also noted in his study that the grand jury practices a unique form of reverse discrimination favoring defendants. In 1971 alone twelve different grand juries heard 15,930 cases and spent an estimated 1,344 hours deliberating the question of whether to indict or issue a no bill. This yields an average of five minutes per case. Carp's data further suggest that only about 5 percent of all these cases receive careful attention. The problem is magnified by recognizing that fully 46 percent of those defendants that are indicted are eventually dismissed or acquitted (Carp 1974: 90-120).

It is reasonable to assume that the decisions reached by grand juries represent institutional responses to social behaviors that are viewed as desirable or undesirable. Saying that some killings are socially acceptable (but not necessarily desirable) is the equivalent of saying that such acts are positively sanctioned by the culture. The failure to spend the time and human resources, combined with expressions of community concerns over a persistently high rate of interpersonal violence among its members, signals that many killings are viewed as appropriate responses to interference with one's person or property.

That less than half of the killings in Houston led to indictments cannot be soley attributed to the attitudes of grand jury members. These persons, who I think quite accurately gauge what sorts of acts the public disapprove of, also receive direct instructions from the district attorney about the statutory laws that may apply to a particular case under particular circumstances. The codification of negative and organized sanctions in the Texas Penal Code does prescribe specific forms of punishment for specific violations of different criminal statutes. The Texas Penal Code, which has survived 117 years without major changes in the area of the criminal law pertaining to homicide and assault, also embodies a series of positive sanctions which reinforce and indeed permit individuals to use lethal force given specific conditions and circumstances.

Article I, Section 23 of the Constitution of Texas insures: "Every citizen shall have the right to bear arms in the lawful defense of himself or the State...." The right to bear arms, which 200 years ago was established as a special consti- tutional right to insure against the arbitrary actions of a tyrannical government, seems strangely out of place in contemporary American society. The avail- ability of deadly weapons and positive private and public sanctions for their use for self-defense or in the defense of property are indeed a lethal combina- tion. A citizen of Texas is thus permitted by law to employ lethal force in self-defense (and he or she, unlike those in other jurisdictions in the United States, is not required to yield from a dangerous confrontation and only use lethal force in a place of last retreat, in the protection of property (if somebody is observed to be breaking into your car he may be shot, or in the protection of a third person (a person may kill if he observes somebody else using "illegal" force against another person).

The wide latitude accorded private citizens in the use of firearms, or other lethal weapons, to settle problems quite naturally confronts both the police and eventual pacifist grand jury members with a dilemma: the decision whether a person has used legal or illegal force is, in the absence of eyewitnesses, founded on the killer's version of the events leading to the death of his oppon- ent.

The public institutions charged with the negative sanctioning of antisocial and illegal behavior are caught in a peculiar bind. On the one hand, the autho- rities are supposed to bring offenders to justice and to preserve public order. On the other hand, these same authorities operate under guidelines which spell out a series of rights and privileges for persons who may respond lethally under socially and legally approved circumstances. The net result of all this is simply that the justice system tips heavily in favor of the perpetrators of violence. This is as true for Texas as it is for the nation as a whole.

According to the most recently published tabulation of homicide statistics by the FBI, "Law enforcement agencies' reports disclose that 55 percent of all adults arrested for murder in 1975 were prosecuted during the year. Fifty-four percent of the adults prosecuted were found guilty as charged, and 14 percent were convicted of some lesser charge. The remaining won release by acquittal or dismissal of the charges against them" (FBI 1976: 20). The FBI further reports that the clearance rate for homicide cases, nationwide, has decreased from 86 percent to 78 percent since the year 1970. Since the official and national homicide rate in 1975 rose to an all-time high of 20,510, or 9.6 known victims per 100,000 population, which in itself represents a 125 percent increase in homicide over the year 1960, it is evident that the number of persons

who commit homicide and go unpunished not only remains at a high level but
that killers are becoming more numerous in the population as a whole.

## The Cultural Context of Homicidal Behavior

Homicide is a cultural universal. No known society escapes violent forms of
human interaction and no society can insure complete personal safety for its
members. It is also evident from cross-cultural data that the relative level of
interpersonal violence in any given society is a function of the "cultural guidelines" which specify precisely the circumstances under which violence may be
used as a means to achieve some end. In modern complex societies we usually
look directly for the institutionalized sanctions found in various legal codes
and court decisions to discover how a particular society sanctions the use of
personal violence. While it is possible that legal institutions may only vaguely
mirror community values, it cannot be said that legal institutions are detached
from the culture as a whole. The complex relationships between individual
social conduct and institutional mechanisms for the regulation of such conduct
are well known to all of us. And it is, of course, impossible here to do more
than call attention to the existence of these relationships. I shall argue, however, that institutional concepts about desirable and undesirable forms of
homicide closely reflect cultural values and sanctions.

There is no hard evidence, from Houston or elsewhere, that would permit
the conclusion that individuals who employ violent means to achieve some
personal goal specifically know how their behavior will be perceived and eval-
uated by other members of the society. Our cultural fascination with murder
mysteries, which represent intellectual puzzles and unconscious aggression,
reflects a general interest in cases that involve killers who carefully calculate
the relative risks of their behavior in relationship to the achievement of their
murderous goals. The Hill murder case falls in this category because the
alleged murderer (Dr. Hill) could have disposed of his disagreeable wife in
such a way that neither the medical nor the judicial authorities could attribute
the woman's death to his act. The Hill case, in other words, challenged the
legal authorities because they suspected, or were carefully led to suspect by
other interested parties, that Mrs. Hill had actually been murdered by an
intelligent but devious husband. The vast majority of homicides in this
country very much lack the puzzling elements illustrated by the Hill murder
case. "Ordinary" murder cases receive much less attention and, ultimately,
reflect how values enable cultural participants to discriminate among acts of
violence as desirable, undesirable, or as unremarkable events of city life.

How, then, does the individual citizen know what degree of violent behavior
he might be able to get away with? Most citizens neither read nor fully under-

stand the convoluted language of criminal statutes. Statutory laws are not written by laymen for laymen but carefully formulated by lawyers for lawyers. Yet it is laymen, and principally those at the bottom of the educational and socioeconomic pyramid, that make up the bulk of those who use killing and assault to resolve conflicts. This situation represents less of a paradox than it may seem. An ordinary citizen will perceive what forms of behavior are acceptable and unacceptable to the authorities and their fellow citizens by observing how other people behave and how the authorities treat those who use violence. A person in Houston does not have to consult the daily papers to find out what somebody else may have gotten away with. He can directly observe persons in his environment who have acted violently and who, in turn, have been apprehended and released by the authorities. More indirect knowledge of law, as in the case of the cuckold, is also transmitted through the process of acculturation. The behavior of the cheated husband was deliberate and premeditated. His disposal of his wife's paramour was well within the technical boundaries of the Texas Penal Code (the provision of the Texas Penal Code which allows a husband the legal privilege to kill his wife and her paramour if he catches both in the act of adulterous intercourse has been eliminated from the new 1974 Texas Penal Code). The behavior of the irate husband, by local standards and by his own arrogant admissions at the scene of the killing, was viewed as a form of gallantry. He did, after all, not bother to shoot his wife, which would have been legally permissible under the circumstances.

Where, we might ask, did the irate motorist pick up the idea that he was somehow justified in: 1) arming himself with a hunting knife while approaching a fellow motorist and 2) using the same knife to take another human life because the other person offended him by making a "threatening" gesture to "get his own knife"? The killer must have drawn upon his knowledge of cultural sanctions because he correctly anticipated the symbolic significance of the other persons's behavior as a threat which could be met with equal or superior force. Whether he believed that he was being subjected to mortal attack, and therefore did not have to yield his ground, is quite irrelevant. He assumed, on the basis of his personal knowledge of his culture, that he was privileged to use lethal force on this occasion. The subsequent action of the grand jury could only reinforce this belief by raising his assumption to the level of legal principle. His wife, mistress, and all other persons connected with the events of this case would also be reinforced in their beliefs about the appropriateness of killing under similar circumstances.

The case of the two stripteasers would undoubtedly, if the killer had stayed in the apartment and called the police, have resulted in the issue of a no bill. The fact that the two women attempted to conceal the act (temporarily) by clumsily attempting to dispose of the body may have led the grand jury to issue an indictment. The trial court, however, must have dismissed these circumstances as insufficient evidence for a conviction. It may be assumed that the element of self-defense (that is, the two principals presumably struggled over the .38 caliber pistol used in the killing) called forth enough doubts in the jurors to warrant acquittal. Yet it does seem unusual that a person who acts in self-defense, especially in a community where self-defense with weapons is a respectable and common form of behavior, should go to such great lengths to disguise the homicide from the police. Would not, in other less permissive jurisdictions, the expertise and coolness of attitude exhibited by this woman enticed a district attorney to at least seek indictment for a lesser charge (such as the obstruction of justice) along with the charge of criminal or negligent homicide? We are left to speculate about these matters and must simply recognize one fact: a man was killed and his killer went unpunished.

## Conclusions

There still is no consensus among behavioral scientists, even when they look at the same data, on the reasons why so many Americans annually kill each other. Different explanations of the nation's high homicide rate have traditionally been attributed to a variety of factors: the historical continuation of the frontier mentality into the twentieth century, the discrimination against racial minorities and disadvantaged socioeconomic groups, or the psychological frustrations of life in large, impersonal cities. The federal government, state governments, and citizens have been equally frustrated not only in explaining violence but in curtailing it in any significant way. Texas, which over the years has recorded more homicides and fewer convictions per capita than most other states, provides but one example of how the total cutural context of violence must be studied and understood before action can be taken to curtail the increasing level of interpersonal violence in the populace.

The extrapolation of findings from Houston to other major U.S. cities must, of course, take into account such variables as regional differences in statutory laws and variations in public attitudes toward violence. The successful legislation of gun control laws by one state legislature quite obviously will be ineffective unless other states adopt similar prohibitions against the personal ownership and use of lethal weapons. It is disconcerting that legal regulations, at both federal and local levels, apply to every activity that American citizens may engage in except to the use of dangerous weapons. The curtailment of violence must clearly begin with the elimination of the means of violence. Other more profound social changes will undoubtedly require major efforts to reform those aspects of the total cultural system that threaten civilized life.

## References

Carp, Robert A. The Harris County Grand Jury—A Case Study. *Houston Law Review,* 12 (1974): 90-120.

Federal Bureau of Investigation. Crime in the United States: Uniform Crime
    Reports: 1975. Washington, D.C.: Government Printing Office, 1976.
Kluckholn, Clyde, and Kelley, William H. The Concept of Culture. In *The
    Science of Man in the World Crisis,* edited by Ralph Linton. New York:
    Columbia University Press, 1945, pp. 78-106.
Lundsgaarde, Henry P. *Murder in Space City: A Cultural Analysis of Houston
    Homicide Patterns.* New York: Oxford University Press, 1977. Reprinted
    with permission.
Thompson, Thomas. *Blood and Money.* New York: Doubleday and Company,
    Inc., 1976.

# 6 Black Women and Homicide

*Maxine Letcher*

## Introduction

The past few years have witnessed a steep rise in the number of reported acts of violence throughout the country. Explanations for this phenomenon are being sought in many quarters, by scholars, law enforcement officials, and, of course, concerned citizens. The most serious of these acts, homicide, has shared in this increase and is viewed with particular alarm in the black community since blacks comprise slightly over one-half of the victims (10,817 out of 21,465 in 1974), but make up only about 11 percent of the population. The disproportionate number of blacks who are victims of lethal violence is obvious from the most cursory glance at homicide statistics. Taking a somewhat closer look, it becomes apparent that young black men between the ages of fifteen and twenty-four are being victimized at a particularly high rate. Some attention has been devoted to these disquieting facts in the social science literature, although there is still very little consensus regarding causal factors.

There have been even fewer successful attempts to explain feminine behavior as it relates to acts of lethal violence, and the literature on black women in this area is virtually nonexistent. Perhaps this apparent lack of interest is accounted for by the relatively small numbers of females involved in this behavioral sequence. In 1974, for example, out of 21,465 homicide victims, 5,718 were women. The circumstances under which females are involved in homicide differ somewhat from those involving males. Men, probably as a result of their broader networks outside of the home, are more likely to be killed by a close friend. The overwhelming majority of women are killed by a family member or lover. When women turn the tables and kill, they are more likely to kill a husband or lover than any other person (Goode, 1969). Given the limited previous treatment of violence as a cause of death among women, this essay will focus on patterns of violence among this subpopulation with special emphasis on black women and their patterns of involvement in lethal violence. There are a number of traditional models which have attempted to explain female victimization and aggression as an outgrowth of their perceived sex roles. An evaluation of the usefulness of these models will form the core of this paper.

Data describing black women homicide victims in Detroit in 1970 will be used to formulate hypotheses which may be generally applicable. In 1974, national figures indicate that the homicide rate—the number of victims per 100,000

population—for black women was more than four times as great as that for
white women.

In 1975, 577 persons died in Detroit as a result of the commission of acts of
lethal violence. Of these, 478 were male and ninety-three were female. Four
hundred thirty-four of the total number were black. Black females were killed
more than twice as often as white ones (sixty-five blacks and twenty-eight whites,
respectively). As one would expect, the overwhelming majority of the victims
were born in the state of Michigan. However, a large number of black women
were born in the states of Alabama, Mississippi, Georgia, and Tennessee. With
both men and women slightly more of the victims were married or separated as
opposed to being single. The weapon used in the overwhelming majority (75.5
percent) of cases was a handgun; following in a distant second place was a knife
(12.4 percent). An interesting difference between men and women emerges from
the data on age. Men's victimization rates peak between ages 20-24 and decline
in all age categories after that. Women in the same range also experience high
levels of victimization, but the highest levels occur in the 35-39 age category
(Detroit Department of Public Health). Data from other years would need to be
examined in order to determine whether this observation is stable over time.

## Homicide Cases

Although police reports of homicides are, for the social scientist's purposes,
quite sketchy, they do contain some valuable information. In order to give the
reader a sense of what these reports contain, a few involving black female victims
will be presented below. They have been chosen because each represents a trend
or a theoretically significant issue.

In the first case, a twenty-six-year-old woman involved in a common-law
relationship with her thirty-one-year-old attacker had a domestic quarrel. He
threatened her with a hammer and a .38 caliber revolver. Ultimately he entered
the bathroom, where she was fixing her hair, and fired a shot at her, striking her
chest. The defendant was found guilty of second-degree murder by a jury and
was sentenced to fourteen to twenty years (Detroit Police Department, 1975).

In this case the couple was married. The woman, who was thirty-eight, and
her husband, thirty-seven, "became involved in a family argument." The husband
was apparently convinced that the woman had a boyfriend and was cheating on
him. "He became so enraged that he beat her with his fists, kicked her, and beat
her with a piece of rubber hose, until she became unconscious." The coroner
declared that the cause of death was multiple traumatic injuries of the body."
The defendant pled guilty to manslaughter and was sentenced to five years'
probation and fined $500 court costs (Detroit Police Department, 1975).

Another married couple were involved in a homicide followed by a suicide.
The woman, thirty-two, was found sitting in a car with a gunshot wound in her

temple. The husband, thirty-seven, was found on his back next to the car. Both were dead at the scene of the crime. The couple had returned from a party and were apparently parking the car when the incident occurred. The defendant who had committed suicide was charged with first-degree murder (Detroit Police Department, 1975).

A seventy-two-year-old man was found guilty of stabbing his thirty-two-year-old girl friend in the abdomen, back, and arms. The coroner found that it was the stab wounds to the abdomen that had proved fatal. In this case it was found by the police that the woman had pushed the defendant during an argument. He pulled a kitchen knife from his coat and stabbed her several times. He pled guilty to manslaughter and was sentenced to from ten to fifteen years in prison (Detroit Police Department, 1975).

Another type of family situation occurred when a mother who was fifty-four was killed by her son, twenty-nine. The son was visiting on a two-day permit from the state hospital. He became embroiled in a quarrel with his mother, went to her bedroom, got a gun, and shot her with it. He was ruled insane and sent to an institution for eighteen months.

The final case involves a thirty-six-year-old woman who was killed by burglars. The deceased went to the rear of her house, where four men had been seen. Several shots were heard. The woman's assailants were later identified in a lineup as the men who were in back of the house at the time of the shooting. Two of them were found guilty of manslaughter and sentenced to three to fifteen and seven to fifteen years in prison, respectively (Detroit Police Department, 1975).

The above-described cases have been presented in order to provide the reader with a sense of the circumstances surrounding lethal violence involving black women. Attention will now be turned to possible explanations of why black women are more frequently involved, both as victims and offenders, in acts of lethal violence than white women.

## Concepts Used to Explain Female Behavior

A place to start in considering which theoretical statements are relevant is with the most general all-encompassing approach. For this we turn to the ideas and concepts contained in the popular thesis of a subculture of violence. This conceptual approach would account for black women being both victims and perpetrators of homicide by postulating that the women belong to this subculture.

The central thesis in the loosely structured assumptions concerned with the subculture of violence—that a set of rules and norms defining situations in which violence is acceptable are different from those of the mainstream culture—operates to influence behavior in the subculture (Ferracuti and Wolfgang, 1969).

Although these ideas do not refer exclusively to lethal violence surely it can be included in the discussion as a type of violence. By the norms defined by this subculture, members of it feel little remorse for their violent behavior and the converse of violence, nonviolence, is punished.

There are several weaknesses associated with this approach. For example, what are its defining variables? Some have suggested that southernness is such a variable (Gastil, 1971). Similarly race has been associated with the concept (Goode, 1969:948). However, certain problems are apparent upon reflection on these points. Surely membership in a culture of violence cannot be defined solely along racial lines, nor do Ferracuti and Wolfgang indicate such. It is well known that violence is denounced by a segment of the black population, for such is reflected in the rise of Dr. Martin Luther King's nonviolence movement during the late 1950s. Further, there are numerous Christian-derived folk beliefs advocating nonviolence which blacks allude to frequently. While these may be prescriptions of ideal culture and not reflected in real culture, no systematic inquiry into this matter has yet been made. In fact Dr. King, far from being considered a cultural deviant, is accorded a respect bordering on awe. Mere southernness does not satisfactorily explain the existence of a subculture of violence since lethal violence is increasing among individuals born and reared in the North.

Rather than postulating a difficult-to-define subculture of violence it might be more fruitful to examine what influence or potential the mainstream culture has on individuals who commit violent acts. Such a line of inquiry would obviate the need for distinguishing between the main culture and the subculture and avoid inappropriate pigeonholing or stereotyping of a large group of people.

Models of violent behavior are frequently seen in mainstream, middle-class, American culture. Television, for example, is designed at enormous industry cost to reach the maximum number of people. The recent Surgeon General's report on television violence has revealed that a child by the age of ten will have witnessed thousands of homicide events. Research is needed to ascertain the effects of constantly viewing such a level of violence on those reared with a steady diet of television. This is particularly relevant to the study of lethal violence because blacks and lower-class persons, both involved disproportionately in homicide, watch more television than others.

Another set of attitudes drawn from the larger American culture concerns possession of firearms. Many Americans believe that the Constitution guarantees the right to own a gun and that it is acceptable to kill another person for a crime against property or in self-defense. There are numerous other examples in American culture of acceptance of an ethos of violence, however the above-mentioned examples suffice to make the point that models of violence which may influence behavior are pervasive and not necessarily subcultural.

## Black Women

In looking for explanations for the black female's being involved more often in acts of lethal violence than white women, a review of commonly held American attitudes about her may lead to theoretically profitable lines of inquiry. American culture does have well-developed attitudes concerning black women. Some grow out of the unique history of blacks in this country. Others are an extension of attitudes applied to white women. One familiar stereotype is that of the mammy—a large, asexual but nurturant woman who is a faithful servant. This type presents a quietly suffering, nonchallenging and unthreatening image to the world. In the 1940s and earlier, it was virtually impossible for an aspiring black actress to find employment who did not conform physically to this mammy image. Lena Horne speaks poignantly about this imagery in her autobiography (Horne, 1966).

The opposite image is one of a mystically sensual creature approachable for the most part in questionable circumstances for purely hedonistic purposes and certainly not to be included in polite society but rather to be discussed at stag affairs and the like. This stereotype has almost satanic overtones, the woman being considered a force of evil which must be struggled against.

The behavior of the Amos n' Andy character, Sapphire, is widely thought to reflect an accurate portrait of the black woman. She is portrayed as verbally caustic, specializing in henpecking and harassing men in general, and in addition she is considered physically unattractive.

A common social science stereotype of the black woman is that of a person struggling against all odds to hold a disintegrating family together as either the dominant partner or the sole breadwinner in the household. Often, the mistaken (recent figures have shown that unemployment is highest among black women) viewpoint is held that it is easier for her to find work than it is for a black male. This is said to result in a lessening in male pride and leads to marital difficulties. It is further believed that she possesses educational advantages over the male. These and other characteristics enhance her castrating qualities.

More examples could be provided but the few stereotypical views of the black woman mentioned above suffice to illustrate the point with which we are concerned here. Views commonly held in American culture (often by both whites and blacks) about black women put them in a different category from other women. Although all women are questioning stereotyped images held of them by American culture, there do exist some images of women in mainstream culture that are completely positive. Mother is one of these positive models. Popular stereotypes of the black woman, on the other hand, set her apart from society as a difficult-to-understand creature.

Negative stereotypes of black women are important to understanding the role of black women in homicide.  Reasons why disproportionately more black women are victims of homicide may be found to be related to the general low regard with which they are held in society.  They are most frequently victims of their husbands or lovers (also black), who may share the mainstream culture's low opinion of the black woman and in addition believe that somehow she is the source of their problems as well.  In the cases sketchily presented previously it seems a tenable hypothesis that the judges and juries involved did not perceive that the person who was dead had been important when they sentenced those charged, although a more intensive assessment of these cases would be necessary to verify this hypothesis.

Contrary to those stereotypes holding that black women have many advantages over black men, the truth is that black women have few choices or advantages.  Only 7.6 percent of black women attain a college degree.  Black women's earnings are lower than those of white women even though black women are employed in greater numbers.  They are employed frequently in low-status, low-paying jobs such as operatives or service workers.

The above-mentioned factors and others reinforce the low esteem in which black women are held in American culture.  The extremely stressful circumstances under which the black woman exists will probably be found upon careful study to be highly related to the reasons she commits homicide more frequently than others.

Wolfgang and Ferracuti attempted an explanation of patterns of homicide among black women as offenders.  They state that black women strike out at black men—their most frequent victims—because the women feel inadequately protected by the men (1967:158).  While this may be an interesting hypothesis a great deal more evidence would be required to demonstrate its validity.  It would be necessary to define inadequate protection and to demonstrate that women, when inadequately defended, strike out at those whom society deems their defenders.  This is at best a tenuous assumption and at worst a blatantly sexist one.  In either case it is not an adequate explanation for the patterns of homicide among black female offenders.

Another writer has described the black female homicide offender as being mainly reactive, meaning that most black women commit homicide in self-defense as a reactor in a situation rather than as an initiator.  If this is true, the problem is quite clearly the individual who is threatening the woman—the black man.  This creates the difficulty that black males are then causing their own deaths (Adler, 1975).

Other writers have seen the issue of black female criminality, though not specifically related to homicide, as growing out of historical conditions, particularly those surrounding family life during slavery when the black woman was taken advantage of and used and forced to assume a role of strength in the family.  These and other circumstances blurred sex-role distinctions for the black female and, as one writer says, "forced her to run earlier faster and farther before white women entered the race" (Adler, 1975:153). Thus, continuing in this line of reasoning black women have a greater propensity to commit acts of violence, but white women may be expected to catch up as sex roles become increasingly blurred (Adler, 1975).

The question of why women commit violent crimes has been dealt with by several authors. Simon sums it up interestingly in *Women and Crime* (1976). She notes that it has been hypothesized that women commit crimes of violence as a response to feelings of frustration and victimization. These feelings, she postulates, should decrease as women are better represented in the labor force and as their acquisition of skills increases. At the same time, women should be found to participate more frequently in white-collar offenses such as fraud and embezzlement (Simon, 1975:19). If the hypothesis is correct that women commit crimes of violence as a response to feelings of frustration and victimization then one would expect that crimes of violence among black women should be on the increase. If the concepts of frustration and victimization can be successfully operationalized, research on this question should yield interesting results.

## Conclusion

Finally, we return to the central question posed herein; that is, the validity of the concepts that we have considered in explaining the role of black women in the commission of acts of lethal violence. It is difficult in working with such data to avoid a common problem social scientists have faced, blaming the victim instead of finding an explanation for the behavior under observation. The phenomenon of blaming the victim has been widely discussed. The notion of a subculture of violence seems a variation on this theme, which blames the culture to which the actors belong but does not attempt to isolate the antecedents of that culture. No well-defined chain of causality is presented in these assumptions. This is not to negate completely the validity of the approach, but rather to call for more intensive research linking cultural phenomena and behavioral outcome in a variety of circumstances and social environments. Similarly merely noting that some vague part of black culture accepts the notion of violence, it seems to me, has little explanatory usefulness.

The various stereotypes of black women tend to blame her for her own problems. For instance the stereotype which views her as a castrating creature paints a picture against whom violence is almost justified, and, of course, if her assailant is a member of the subculture of violence, he may be viewed as merely following culturally prescribed norms when he deals with her violently as a response to her offensive ways.

Adler's view that somehow white women will overtake black women in the commission of crimes when sex roles become adequately blurred requires proof that this is the outcome of less well defined sex roles. The notion that black women commit more crimes because they are more independent lacks explanatory power since independence can lead to many other outcomes. If Simon and others are correct in saying that women commit crimes of violence out of frustration, then the situation for black women is bleak; because, as can be gleaned from the discussion above, circumstances under which black women live are extremely frustrating and stressful.

A model which would explain black female behavior would have to operationalize some of the vaguely defined notions discussed above, such as culture. Since economic factors have been demonstrated to affect levels of lethal violence perhaps increased research on these variables would be a fruitful place to begin (Brenner, 1977).

In sum, then, it seems apparent that the major work of defining and operationalizing variables which are prerequisite to an explanation of black female behavior is yet to be tackled. It is hoped that in the near future these issues will be seriously addressed in the literature.

## References

Adler, Freda. *Sisters in Crime*. New York: McGraw Hill Book Co., 1975.

Brenner, Harvey. *Estimating the Social Costs of National Economic Policy: Implications for Mental Health, and Criminal Aggression*. Washington, D.C.: U.S. Government Printing Office, 1976.

Gastil, Raymond D. Homicide and a Regional Culture of Violence. *American Sociological Review* 36 (1971): 412-427.

Goode, William. *Violence Between Intimates in Crimes of Violence*. Washington, D.C.: U.S. Government Printing Office, 1969.

Horne, Lena, and Schickel, Richard. *Lena*. London: 1966.

Simon, Rita James. *Women and Crime*. Lexington Mass: D.C. Heath and Company, 1975.

U.S. Surgeon General's Scientific Advisory Committee on Television and Social Behavior. *Television and Growing Up: Report to the Surgeon General*. Washington D.C.: U.S. Government Printing Office.

Wolfgang, Marvin E., and Ferracuti, Franco. *The Subculture of Violence: Towards an Integrated Theory of Criminology*. London: Tavistock Publications, 1967.

# 7

## The Availability of Mental Health Services for Dependents of Homicide Victims

*Anna Mitchell Jackson*

Homicide in urban areas overwhelmingly affects people of color, the poor, and the unemployed. These are the same populations for whom mental health services have been the least available and for whom outcome measures of effectiveness are the most equivocal. Victims of violence constitute a particularly underserved group, as do dependents of homicide victims. In this presentation, the incidence of homicide, problems in mental health delivery, probable reactions to loss, models of psychological treatment, and new trends in treatment will be discussed.

The extensiveness of urban violence has been documented in numerous references (Edwards, 1972; Lester, 1973; Myers, 1967; *Statistical Abstracts of the United States*, 1972-74; and Wolfgang, 1969). The incidence of homicide reported for 1974 in the *Statistical Abstracts of the United States* for urban areas was 13.7 persons per 100,000 population for persons fifteen years of age and older. The figures reported for males are much higher than for females, and much higher for people of color than for white individuals. Correspondingly, the figures given for white males were 12.0 per 100,000; for white females, 3.7 per 100,000; for males of color, 101.7 per 100,000; and for females of color, 20.9 per 100,000. The total number of homicides for these groups was, respectively, 7,992 for white males, 2,656 for white females, 8,755 for males of color, and 2,062 for females of color. A total of 21,465 homicides was cited for this year. In the same publication, a breakdown of homicide victims by age also was given. A survey of this information revealed that most deaths occur for persons between the ages of twenty-five and forty-four—29.5 per 100,000 for males and 7.0 per 100,000 for females. The next highest incidence occurs between the ages of fifteen and twenty-four—22.0 per 100,000 for males and 6.3 per 100,000 for females. The number of deaths for males under age fifteen and for ages forty-five to sixty-four are approximately equivalent—16.3 and 16.9 per 100,000, respectively. The data are the same for females—under age fifteen, 4.4 per 100,000 and for ages forty-five to sixty-four, 3.7 per 100,000. From the data presented in the Statistical Abstracts, it can be seen that most victims of homicide are male, and more often black males, and that most tend to be relatively young adults.

Wolfgang (1969) presented very similar information from studies he has conducted. He found that most victims of homicide are between twenty and forty years of age and also that most victims of homicide are male—70 percent.

Further elaborations presented by Wolfgang revealed that most homicides occur among males, approximately 61 percent, and that most perpetrators of homicide are males, or approximately 88 percent. A striking point presented by Wolfgang is that an overwhelmingly large percentage of victims and offenders of homicide are relatives, close acquaintances, or friends, and that most are of the same ethnic group as the offender, approximately 94 percent. It is estimated that only about one-third of all homicides are committed by strangers (Edwards, 1972). Robbery is a common motive in this instance. Robbery homicides have increased more rapidly than other homicides in recent years (Block, 1977, and Zimring, 1977). Another interesting fact presented by Wolfgang is that a high percentage of females over the age of sixteen are killed by their husbands. This occurs in about 50 percent of cases in female homicides.

MacDonald (1961) concurred with many of the basic facts presented above. In his research on violent behavior and dangerousness, he found that the majority of victims tend to be between the ages of twenty-five and thirty-five, that the victim and the perpetrator are of the same race in 94 percent of homicides, and that victims are either close friends or relatives of the murderer. He found also that persons committing homicides tend to be younger than victims, often being between the ages of twenty and thirty. Another factor discussed by MacDonald was the contributory role of the victims. The possible provocative behavior and/or suicidal wishes of victims have been raised by others as well (Wolfgang, 1969). In recent years, the accidental victim of violent crimes has been discussed (Symonds, 1975) and the role of the victim in provoking assaults has been questioned.

The incidence of child homicide victims is presented in part by Myers (1967). The study he reports was conducted in Detroit, Michigan, between 1940 and 1965. A total of eighty-three child homicides were documented during this period. Parents were found to be responsible in 60 percent of the cases. Familiarity with the assailant prior to the homicide was found in almost all instances. A large number of the children killed were under the age of three— 46 percent. In instances where parents committed the homicidal act, a high percentage, 42 percent, were overtly psychotic. Impulsive rage in response to behavior exhibited by the child, such as excessive crying, was the next most frequent motive.

To use Wolfgang's term, "who kills whom" is reasonably evident as well as who is killed. What is not as evident is what services are provided on a consistent basis for persons who exhibit violent behavior and for persons who are victims of that behavior. By and large, dependents of homicide victims seem to be an especially neglected group. The dearth of services for this group may be associated with a number of factors: the availability of resources and personnel; the recognition of the need for services; differing opinions about what should be provided and when; economic factors; and political and social policies, to mention a few.

Pasternack (1975), in his book *Violence and Victims*, presented original works of persons who have been engaged in the research and treatment of individuals who demonstrate dangerous behavior and those who have been the recipients of that behavior. In this connection, Lion described a violence clinic that was developed to treat persons exhibiting violent outbursts. Lion discussed several items that were found to be associated with violent outbursts. Prominent among these were perceived threats of separation or loss and fear of abandonment. Intensification of these feelings resulted in physical attack and possibly homicidal behavior. Other factors described by Lion for males treated at the center were negative thoughts about significant persons—for example, family members—which were suppressed. The need to defend against the negative feelings was thought to be supported by the fact that violent acts occurred frequently in conjunction with negative comments about family members, made by others. Lion and his associates thought that facilitating verbal mediation by having violence-prone individuals give detailed descriptions and thoughts of violent incidents would help decrease violent outbursts. Treatment also consisted of teaching the individuals to fantasize and to recognize and label feelings.

In the same book, Symonds (1975) discussed reactions of persons who are accidental victims of violent crimes such as robbery, rape, and kidnapping, as well as reactions that nonvictims have to them. In the latter instance, he listed three probable responses of nonvictims to victims: assumptions about complicity of the victim in the incident, for example, as a stimulator of the assault; isolation and exclusion of the victim; and indifference to the plight of the victim. These responses, coupled with the trauma of the incident itself, he thought, may lead to increased feelings of shock, fear, rage, vulnerability, and lack of trust. He felt that treatment approaches must take into account these responses, especially the feelings of loss and the new status of the victim.

The suggestions made by Lions and Symonds are not unlike those made by clinicians and researchers who describe the mourning or bereavement process. Gassem (1975) and Smith (1975) concur, as do others, that grief or mourning must accompany actual loss or feelings of loss if personal growth and/or adjustment is to continue. Lindbergh (1973) added that the person must accept the notion that vulnerability is an implicit part of attachments and be willing to take that risk. The stronger the attachment, the more intense the feelings of loss. All describe the stages of the mourning process: depression; denial; acknowledgment of the loss; grief; and the ability to form new attachments.

Depression or the feeling of profound sadness, hopelessness, helplessness, and apathy is the first stage of bereavement. In this stage, the individual feels overwhelmed by the loss and is still quite attached to the lost object or person. The individual may find himself or herself thinking of the lost person as if the person were still alive or may even imagine that the dead person is seen—that is, hallucinate images of the deceased individual. This profound depression is accompanied frequently by lack of appetite, sleeplessness, restlessness, and by decrease in weight. Prolonged depression often is accompanied by suicidal

ideation or suicidal gestures. The normal depression stage in mourning is relatively brief—a few weeks. Depression which lasts past this period may be cause
for concern. Guilt feelings are frequent components of depression. These occur
in conjunction with negative thoughts which may have occurred in relation to
the lost object.

The depressive stage is usually followed by denial of the loss. In this stage,
the person clings to the hope that a mistake has been made and that the individual presumed dead is in fact alive. Elaborate fantasies may be invoked to
reinforce these beliefs. Again, this stage tends to be relatively brief in the normal
mourning process.

Acknowledgment of the loss occurs gradually after the denial process is
spent. In this phase, the person begins to talk about the deceased individual in
the past tense and is able to get in touch with ambivalent feelings that might
have been associated with that individual. This acknowledgment lays the foundation for the actual grief that follows in rapid order. The grieving process may
last for some time unless it is facilitated by supportive individuals. Successful
mourning allows the person to decrease the strength of attachment to the lost
object and frees them to form new bonds and relationships. Interests are re-
vitalized, adaptive functioning is improved, and a positive outlook is restored.

The mourning process is necessarily different for children than for adults.
In fact, considerable controversy exists as to whether or not children can mourn
(Schowalter, 1975, and Tallmer, 1975). It is commonly accepted that children
do not fully comprehend the meaning of death until age nine. This lack of
capacity is thought to be associated with limitations in cognitive ability as well
as with the painful nature of the loss itself. Also, children are involved in very
dependent relationships with adults, a fact which intensifies the qualitative
experience of the loss. What happens often is that the child will identify with the
lost object even more and will often idealize the deceased person. An image
of the lost individual will be maintained until such time as development pro-
gresses sufficiently so that mourning can occur. This is thought to be in adolescence (Schowalter, 1975), when emotional separation as well as alterations of
attachments can occur. Responses to death vary with the age of the child. In
infants, withdrawal, apathy, and anaclitic depression usually result. In preschool-
and school-age children, sleep and feeding disturbances as well as excitability,
school failure, behavior problems, and delinquency may result. Phobias may
occur if prolonged illness preceded the death of the primary-care provider.
Intense feelings of guilt may occur if death of the significant adult was the result
of suicide.

Since depression, possible suicidal ideation, and possible maladjustment
may accompany experiences of loss, intervention at the time of the loss has been
recommended by a number of clinicians. Danto (1975) suggested that resources
along a number of lines be made available immediately, for example, financial
assistance and free counseling. Welu (1975) suggested that psychotherapy be

provided within two days. Persons usually in contact with survivors, such as ministers, were seen as logical persons to provide these services with appropriate training by mental health professionals. Silverman (1975) described a special program developed for widows in which other widows served as support persons for persons in a similar position. In this instance, widows contacted other widows soon after the deaths of their husbands and remained available to them on a continuing basis. Caroff and Dobrof (1975) described family psychotherapy following a loss. However, these interventions and preventive measures often were innovations rather than routine approaches or service offered to "survivor-victims" as Welu (1975) describes them.

Basic mental health approaches involve secondary or tertiary rather than preventive care. The traditional contact occurs when the person in need of services, or an agency on behalf of that person or family, alerts the mental health facility. When this occurs, the services offered are directly related to the theoretical or philosophical orientation of that setting. Typical approaches involve psychodynamic (psychoanalytically oriented), behavioral, cognitive, or crisis intervention methods. Increasingly, self-directed and self-help approaches are being used.

Psychodynamic approaches may involve either individual, group, or family treatment. One of the basic premises in this approach is that internal conflicts in response to external stress pose interferences with adaptive behavior. The treatment typically consists of the development of insight into the factors instrumental in the formation of the conflict and the concomitant development of alternative behaviors which lead to more adaptive responses. In individual treatment, the relationship with the therapist is used as the major vehicle for change. The relationship variable remains as the crucial element in group and family treatment as well. However, in these instances, the experiences of other persons act as support and as verification that similar experiences that the individual is having occur as a rule in traumatic incidents.

Behavior modification approaches rely on observable responses and to factors which maintain or enhance maladaptive reactions. The importance of social aspects has been incorporated into contingency management of late. As it pertains to reactions to loss, efforts would be made to increase the responsiveness to others by reinforcing interest and physical closeness, that is, by facilitating the attachment to a substitute person. Fear, anxiety, or other affective reactions would be decreased through nonreinforcement or through matching with incompatible responses which would inhibit that behavior. Feelings of hopelessness and helplessness would be combated by the introduction of activities that the individual could successfully accomplish.

Cognitive approaches rely on the development of conscious understanding of what has caused a disruption in coping behavior. Fallacies in thinking are uncovered as well as unsubstantiated facts which are accepted as true. As it pertains to loss, contrary thoughts that a person had about the deceased individual would be pointed out, not as warring factions, but as typical ideas which are present in most relationships. This would hopefully alleviate feelings of guilt and would facilitate mourning.

Crisis intervention has as its goal the reinstitution of the precrisis coping abilities. Efforts would be made in this instance to reestablish or strengthen supportive systems so that adaptive processes can resume effectively. The involvement of mental health professionals is time limited, usually lasting for six to eight contacts. Persons other than the immediate family may be involved in this effort.

New service approaches entail minimal contact of mental health professionals, or in some cases, no contact at all. Self-directed approaches, as the name suggests, involve the use of programmed reading materials by individuals to further adaptive behavior on their own once initial contacts with professionals have been completed, or may be used in conjunction with professional sessions on a limited basis. Recently, peer self-help groups have been started for a variety of problem areas. These often are organized and led in the absence of professional input. Many of these groups are held at cultural or community centers or at churches. Professional consultants may be called upon from time to time, but as a rule, the groups function without this type of consultation.

Except in the few instances described above, mental health services commence only after the plight of the individual becomes known to professional agencies or centers, and then frequently only when more severe psychopathology is being exhibited. It has not been traditional that mental health services have been provided on a routine basis around traumatic losses. Normal grieving mechanisms have been expected to occur semiautomatically and to restore adequate pretraumatic functioning. Current information suggests that this is not the case and that planned, systematic preventive actions is highly desirable.

Possible interferences with normal grief reactions have been alluded to above. Also referred to above are factors which decrease the availability of services. Further elaborations of these points will be presented at this time.

Factors which may interfere with usual mourning reactions include the traumatic aspects of the death of the victim, the age, sex, and developmental levels of the survivor or survivors, the nature of the relationship the survivor(s) had with the victim, and social/cultural elements. Intensification of typical behaviors results in almost all of these instances.

Traumatic deaths frequently lead to complications in mourning. Deaths which occur through violent acts appear to be especially bothersome for surviving next of kin. Important elements leading to complications involve the precipitous nature in which the death occurred, which often maximizes individual feelings, shock, and vulnerability and which may bolster denial processes as a defense against these painful feelings. Fear, numbness, shock, and disbelief are as a rule exacerbated by trauma. Individuals may completely block out what has transpired and/or be oblivious to what is going on around them for prolonged periods of time. In the temporary chaos and disorganization in families accompanying such deaths, these behaviors may be disregarded by persons in a position to help.

The age, sex, and developmental level of persons who are survivors may also influence the mourning process. The capacity to mourn prior to adolescence has been questioned. The finality of death is not understood before age eight or nine. The ability to express anger in response to feelings of abandonment and loss is often abortive because of the physical and emotional importance the deceased person had in the child's life. Basic barriers to mourning in children are thought to be associated with immature development and environmental dependency. It has been reported that early parent loss may be responded to by the child as if part of the self must be denied, the positive/satisfying parts which are introjects of the deceased parent. When this occurs, low self-esteem and acting-out behavior may result. Since the mother, the person who plays a major nurturing role may be killed, heightened needs for dependency may also occur. Girls may have a more difficult time with this loss then boys because of the formers' usual closer relationship with the mother, social roles, and expectations, especially those associated with the expression of anger, the reinforcement of dependency, and the loss of a like identification figure. Men and boys, on the other hand, are expected to demonstrate behavior that inhibits expressions of grief. The nature of the relationship with the deceased also may be a complicating factor. We have seen from the data presented that persons killed tend to be relatives or friends. This suggests that very close relationships frequently exist. The closer the relationship, usually the stronger the bond or attachment, and the more personal the experience of loss.

Differences exist in provisions for mourning along sociocultural lines. Provisions run the gamut from very little outward manifestation to specified mourning periods and encouragement of overt behavior signifying the profoundness of the loss. Religious practices differ also on expected responses for mourners.

A number of other factors could be presented which may lead to complications of the mourning process. However, the ones mentioned are sufficient to point out potential problem areas and to demonstrate the need for intervention and services. Let us now examine why these services may not have been provided.

The availability of services in general is influenced by one's socioeconomic level, power, and political clout. Persons who can exercise authority and power, and who already have resources, are the ones for whom services of any kind are the most available. Again, we have seen from the data on homicides that persons most likely to be affected by homicides are not affluent, powerful individuals, but poor people and people of color. The accessibility of the necessary private resources is beyond the means of many of these individuals. Reliance on public services is, in fact, the usual state of affairs, services which are highly susceptible to changes in federal, state, and local policies and to cutbacks in expenditures. Demonstration of need in this context does not necessarily eventuate in the development of services. Rather, economic resources, as well as political and policy decisions, dictate to a large extent what will develop, where it will be developed, and who will benefit.

In addition to economic, political, and social policies, the development and availability of services are associated both with extant beliefs regarding which needs should receive priority and also with existing demands on facilities and personnel. The most pressing demands, as it pertains to violent acts, traditionally have been associated with the services available to the perpetrators of those acts, not to victims or dependents of victims. Primary prevention in almost any area has been obfuscated by presses for services of persons already in dire straits. It is only recently, then, that attention has been turned to these groups and efforts have been made to directly assist them.

Services, when available, are generally provided by community mental health centers, neighborhood health facilities, cultural and community centers, churches, and self-help groups. In some instances, special clinics have been organized to offer services, some of which have already been described. The availability of these services can be determined by contacting local mental health officials, state associations or mental health organizations, and religious organizations. Increasingly, mental health professionals are volunteering time to consult with neighborhood and community centers and church groups in the interest of public welfare and the promotion of optimal care. Names of these individuals can be obtained through state and national societies, such as the National Association of Black Psychologists, the American Psychological Association, the American Psychiatric Association, the Association of Psychiatric Social Workers, and similar groups.

In this presentation, several things have been attempted. An attempt has been made to delineate the extent of urban violence, specifically homicide, to briefly describe the individuals and groups most likely to be affected by violence, to identify some of the reactions of persons experiencing violence and loss, to review treatment approaches to loss, to specify potential barriers and problems involved in service delivery, and to discuss current and potential resources for services. Current trends in mental health, such as the formation of self-directed and self-help groups, were presented also, as were certain innovations in treatment.

Urban violence affects many people. It is time that attention be turned to those who are most intimately affected; it is time that support, direction, and assistance be offered on a routine basis.

### References

Block, R. Patterns of victim-offender relation and interaction in violent crime. Presented at the Conference on the Lethal Aspects of Urban Violence, University of Wisconsin-Milwaukee, May 1977.

Caroff, P. and Dobrof, R. The helping process with bereaved families. In B. Schoenberg, I. Gerber, A. Wiener, A.H. Kutscher, D. Peretz, and A.C. Carr, eds. *Bereavement: Its Psychosocial Aspects.* New York: Columbia University Press, 1975, pp. 232-242.

Danto, B.L. Bereavement of the widows of slain police officers. In B. Schoenberg, I. Gerber, A. Wiener, A.H. Kutscher, D. Peretz, and A.C. Carr, eds. *Bereavement: Its Psychosocial Aspects.* New York: Columbia University Press, 1975, pp. 150-153.

Edwards, G. Murder and gun control. *The American Journal of Psychiatry,* 1972, 128(7), 811-814.

Gassem, N.H. Bereavement as indispensable for growth. In B. Schoenberg, I. Gerber, A. Wiener, A.H. Kutscher, D. Peretz, and A.C. Carr, eds. *Bereavement: Its Psychosocial Aspects.* New York: Columbia University Press, 1975, pp. 9-17.

Lester, D. Murder: A review. *Journal of Applied Behavior Therapy*, 1973, 13(4), 40-50.

Lindbergh, A.M. *Hour of Gold, Hour of Lead.* New York: Harcourt, 1973.

Lion, J.R. Developing a violence clinic. In S.A. Pasternack, ed. *Violence and Victims.* New York: Spectrum Publications, Incorporated, 1975, pp. 77-78.

MacDonald, J.M. *The Murderer and His Victim.* Springfield, Illinois: Charles C. Thomas, 1961.

Myers, S.A. The child slayer: A 25 year survey of homicides involving preadolescent victims. *Archives of General Psychiatry,* 1967, 17(2), 211-213.

Pasternack, S.A. ed. *Violence and Victims.* New York: Spectrum Publications, 1975.

Schowalter, J.E. Parent death and child bereavement. In B. Schoenberg, I. Gerber, A. Wiener, A.H. Kutscher, D. Peretz, and A.C. Carr, eds. *Bereavement: Its Psychosocial Aspects.* New York: Columbia University Press, 1975, pp. 172-179.

Silverman, P.R., and Silverman, S.M. Withdrawal in bereaved children. In B. Schoenberg, I. Gerber, A. Wiener, A.H. Kutscher, D. Peretz, and A.C. Carr, eds. *Bereavement: Its Psychosocial Aspects.* New York: Columbia University Press, 1975, pp. 208-214.

Smith, J.H. On the work of mourning. In B. Schoenberg, I. Gerber, A. Wiener, A.H. Kutscher, D. Peretz, and A.C. Carr, eds. *Bereavement: Its Psychosocial Aspects.* New York: Columbia University Press, 1975, pp. 18-25.

Symonds, S. The accidental victim of violent crime. In S.A. Pasternack, ed. *Violence and Victims.* New York: Spectrum Publications, Incorporated, 1975, pp. 91-99.

Tallmer, M. Sexual and age factors in childhood bereavement. In B. Schoenberg, I. Gerber, A. Wiener, A.H. Kutscher, D. Peretz, and A.C. Carr, eds. *Bereavement: Its Psychosocial Aspects.* New York: Columbia University Press, 1975, pp. 164-171.

Tanay, E. Psychiatric aspects of homicide prevention. *American Journal of Psychiatry*, 1972, 128(7), 815-818.

U.S. Bureau of the Census, *Statistical Abstract of the United States: 1976*, 97th Edition. Washington, D.C., 1976.

Welu, T.C. Pathological bereavement: A plan for its prevention. In B. Schoenberg, I. Gerber, A. Wiener, A.H. Kutscher, D. Peretz, and A.C. Carr, eds. *Bereavement: Its Psychosocial Aspects*. New York: Columbia University Press, 1975, pp. 139-149.

Wolfgang, M.E. Who kills whom. *Psychology Today*, October 1969, 3(5), 54-56, 72-75.

Zimring, F.E. Determinants of the death rate from robbery: A Detroit time study. Presented at the Conference on the Lethal Aspects of Urban Violence, University of Wisconsin-Milwaukee, May 1977.

# About the Contributors

**Dr. Ruth E. Dennis** is associate professor in the Department of Psychiatry and assistant professor in the Department of Family and Community Health at Meharry Medical College in Nashville, Tennessee. She is director of the Division of Behavioral Sciences and of the research unit in the Department of Psychiatry.

**Dr. Felton J. Earls**, a child psychiatrist, is a graduate of the Howard University School of Medicine. He completed his residency in psychiatry at Massachusetts General Hospital. Presently Dr. Earls is an assistant psychiatrist at the Children's Hospital Medical Center in Boston, an instructor in psychiatry at the Harvard Medical School, and a visiting lecturer in health services administration at the Harvard School of Public Health.

**Dr. Anna M. Jackson** is the director of the Children's Diagnostic Center and associate professor of psychiatry at the University of Colorado Medical Center. She has also served as adjunct professor of psychology at the University of Denver and as a member of the graduate faculty at the University of Colorado at Boulder.

**Dr. Maxine Letcher Nimtz** is an assistant professor of anthropology at the University of Wisconsin—Milwaukee. She previously served as chairman of the Department of Afro-American Studies at that university. She is currently on leave of absence from her teaching position.

**Dr. Henry P. Lundsgaarde** is presently a professor of anthropology at the University of Kansas and was previously chairman of the department of anthropology at the University of Houston.

**Dr. Franklin E. Zimring** is professor of law and director of the Center for Studies in Criminal Justice at the University of Chicago. He served as director of research for the Task Force on Firearms, National Commission on the Causes and Prevention of Violence (1968-1969), and as visiting professor of law at the University of Pennsylvania (1972) and at Yale University (1973).

# About the Editor

**Harold M. Rose** is professor of geography and urban affairs at the University of Wisconsin—Milwaukee. He served as the chairman of the graduate program in urban affairs from 1970 to 1977. His interest in urban violence is an outgrowth of his prior research on the attributes of urban black territorial communities. His published works have focused primarily on black residential mobility. In 1974, Dr. Rose was awarded the Van Cleef memorial medal by the American Geographical Society for his contributions to urban geography. In 1976–1977, he served as president of the Association of American Geographers.

Dr. Rose has served as a visiting professor at Washington University, Northwestern University, and the University of California at Los Angeles. In 1971 he was invited by the Polish Academy of Science to lecture at the Institute of Geography at Warsaw.

# Related
# Lexington Books

Richard Block, *Violent Crime*

Ann Wolbert Burgess, A. Nicholas Groth, Lynda Lytle Holmstrom, and
    Suzanne Sgroi, *Sexual Assault of Children and Adolescents*

John P. Conrad and Simon Dinitz, *In Fear of Each Other*

Floyd Feeney, *Holdups, Muggings, and Pursesnatcher*

Jack Goldsmith and Sharon S. Goldsmith, *Crime and the Elderly*

Robert Hermann, Eric Single, and John Boston, *Counsel for the Poor*

James M. McPartland and Edward L. McDill, *Violence in Schools*

Roger E. Meiners, *Victim Compensation*

Charles E. Owens and Michael L. Lindsey, *Mental Health and the Black
    Offender*